DIMENSIONAL ILLUSTRATORS, INC.
SOUTHAMPTON, PENNSYLVANIA

ROCKPORT PUBLISHERS
ROCKPORT, MASSACHUSETTS

DISTRIBUTED BY NORTH LIGHT
CINCINNATI, OHIO

3-DIMENSIONAL ILLUSTRATORS AWARDS ANNUAL II

The

Best

In

3-D Advertising

And

Publishing

Worldwide

ISBN 0-935603-89-1

Produced by Dimensional Illustrators, Inc.
Southampton, Pennsylvania

Published by Rockport Publishers, Inc.
Five Smith Street
Rockport, Massachusetts 01966

Distributed to the book trade and art trade in the U.S.
and Canada by:
North Light, an imprint of Writer's Digest Books
1507 Dana Avenue
Cincinnati, Ohio 45207
Telephone: (513) 531-2222

Distributed to the book trade and art trade
throughout the rest of the world by:
Hearst Books International
1350 Avenue of the Americas
New York, New York 10019
Telephone: (212) 261-6770

Other distribution by:
Rockport Publishers, Inc.
Five Smith Street
Rockport, Massachusetts 01966
Telephone: (508) 546-9590
Fax: (508) 546-7141
Easy Link: 62945477

Address direct mail sales to:
Dimensional Illustrators, Inc.
362 Second Street Pike, Suite 112
Southampton, PA 18966
Telephone: (215) 953-1415
Fax: (215) 953-1697

PRINTED IN HONG KONG

Library of Congress-in-Publication Data

3-DIMENSIONAL ILLUSTRATORS AWARDS ANNUAL II
THE BEST IN 3-D ADVERTISING AND PUBLISHING WORLDWIDE

CREATIVE DIRECTOR/EDITOR
Kathleen Ziegler
Dimensional Illustrators, Inc.

EXECUTIVE EDITOR
Nick Greco
Dimensional Illustrators, Inc.

DESIGNER
Phoebe Darlington-Bush
Hill Design Group, Inc.

SPECIAL THANKS
FOR THEIR LOVE AND SUPPORT
Ann and Bob Ziegler

SPECIAL THANKS
Christa and Michael Greco
Sharon Newman

COVER PHOTOGRAPH
Jim Kelso
Jimé Vance Photographics

COVER ILLUSTRATION
Nancy Blauers
Nancy Blauers Dimensional Illustration
2600 W. Ina Rd. Apt. 256
Tucson, AZ 85741
602-797-2985
203-377-6109

Nancy Blauers is an accomplished 3-Dimensional Illustrator, currently working in Tucson, Arizona. A graduate of The School of Visual Arts, BFA Illustration, Nancy specializes in creating provocative and exotic animals from pine, basswood or terra-cotta clay. Her illustrations are finished in either oils or acrylics. Nancy is a member of The Society of Animal Artists and is the 1989 recipient of the Donald R. Miller Award for Interpretive Sculpture. In 1989 and 1990 respectively, Nancy received Silver and Gold Awards from the Dimensional Illustrators Awards Show. Her work has been exhibited at The Leigh Yawkey Woodson Art Museum, 1990 Wildlife: The Artist's View and 1991, Birds In Art. Clients include Omni Magazine, Globe Books, The Maritime Center at Norwalk, Ballantine Books, Beardsley Zoological Gardens, Playskool and Connecticut Magazine.

The cover illustration, a Black Palm Cockatoo, has a hand carved pine base and individually carved basswood feathers. After sanding and adding fine details with a woodburner, the sculpture was painted in oils. Polyurethane was used to simulate shiny areas of the beak. Realism is added to the sculpture by the use of a glass eye. Nancy's unique style is achieved by familiarizing herself with the subject matter through direct observation, sketches, photos and video. This sculpture was created as an eye-catching self promotion card.

"I am often asked why I choose to express myself through dimensional illustration. My answer is simply that although I love to paint and draw, I feel more at ease and confident expressing myself with chisels and wood. Sculpture as a form of illustration is my way of creatively conveying an idea or depicting subject matter. I feel that Dimensional Illustrators are highly innovative in discovering new and visually stimulating techniques in the illustrative field. It is very exciting for me to be a part of this new wave."

Nancy Blauers

Paper Sculpture
Kathleen Ziegler

C O N T E N T S

PRESIDENT'S MESSAGE

3-Dimensional Illustration is currently experiencing a renaissance in the advertising and publishing community. Art directors increasingly rely on 3-Dimensional Illustrators to solve the myriad of problems facing the communications industry. Creative directors, 3-D illustrators and photographers have combined their talents to form a new partnership. This has resulted in the creation of innovative ads, brochures, posters, magazine covers and editorials that reflect this unique merger of creative talent. Art buyers are experiencing a resurgence throughout the creative market, due to the distinctive union of 3-D image-makers and creative directors. The Gold, Silver and Merit winners demonstrate this extraordinary fusion of technical and conceptual excellence.

As president of Dimensional Illustrators, Inc., I am pleased by the widespread growth and acceptance of 3-Dimensional Illustration. In February of 1991, my partner Nick Greco and I produced the first ever international exhibition of 3-Dimensional Illustration. The 1990 Gold and Silver winners were exhibited at the Fouts and Fowler Gallery in London, England. During this premiere exhibition, visual creatives were given the opportunity to view the work of their colleagues from the United States, Canada and Europe. This international exposure affords 3-Dimensional Illustration the recognition and plaudits it richly deserves.

The winners of the 2nd Annual Dimensional Illustrators Awards Show continue to set the standards of excellence in the burgeoning industry of 3-Dimensional Illustration. The professional quality of each award winning entry is displayed in ***3-Dimensional Illustrators Awards Annual II— The Best In 3-D Advertising And Publishing Worldwide****. Congratulations to all visual creatives for your brilliant application of 3-Dimensional design.*

Kathleen Ziegler
President
Dimensional Illustrators, Inc.

The Art Directors Club Gallery/New York

Fouts & Fowler Gallery/London

New York Exhibition

An estimated 375 guests attended the opening reception of the 2nd Annual Dimensional Illustrators Awards Show. The 1990 show was held at the prestigious Art Directors Club of New York. Visual creatives admired the versatility, depth and professionalism of the 335 award winning entries. Talented creatives from California to Switzerland spent an informal evening reviewing the excellent caliber of 3-Dimensional Illustrations. This year, a student category was added to encourage new young talent within the design community. In addition to the print entries, 3-D animated TV commercials were recognized for their excellence.

London Exhibition

The first ever international Dimensional Illustrators Awards Show was held at the Fouts and Fowler Gallery, in London, England. The establishment of the gallery is the culmination of two decades of acclaim by the communications industry. The Fouts and Fowler Gallery exists in order to, "pursue a wish to achieve more creative freedom." The London opening, showcasing the Gold and Silver winners of the 2nd Annual Dimensional Illustrators Awards Show, was received with great enthusiasm. 3-Dimensional Illustrators from Germany, Scotland, Canada, Denmark and France joined their British colleagues in celebrating the best in 3-Dimensional Illustration from the United States, Canada and Europe.

Kathleen and I wish to thank all the talented professionals and friends for their unwavering support and encouragement. Your continued involvement has helped to promote 3-Dimensional Illustration in the United States and throughout the world.

Nick Greco
Vice President
Dimensional Illustrators, Inc.

"The diversity of material such as paper, metal and yarn, etc. combined with talent make for some extraordinary solutions. I am hopeful that this show will open awareness and appreciation of the 3-Dimensional illustration community to the advertising and design field."

B. MARTIN PEDERSEN

"In my work, I attempt to avoid the typical paper sculpture look in order to achieve artistic freedom, greater imagination and most importantly, a unique style."

AJIN

"There is something 'electric' that happens when a concept is pushed past the conventional media of pencil and paint. It is limited only by the imagination and skill of the dimensional illustrator."

MARGARET CUSACK

"3-Dimensional Illustration, aside from the obvious nature of the term itself, is that type of graphic presentation, using a carefully selected medium that communicates in a visually tactile manner with both rational senses and our emotional hot buttons. The myriad of tones, textures and planes co-ordinate to strike purposefully and with pointed clarity. The result is communication that demands interpretation and emotional response within."

MIKE JAYCOCK

Judging for the 2nd Annual Dimensional Illustrators Awards Show was held the final week of June, 1990, at the Art Directors Club of New York. Judges were chosen for their expertise in the application of 3-Dimensional Illustration and design. Each juror was given the opportunity to evaluate the craftsmanship and overall conceptual design of entries submitted by visual creatives in the advertising and publishing industry.

The selections, chosen by our panel of nationally recognized judges, have assured the success and integrity of the Dimensional Illustrators Awards Show. The Gold, Silver and Merit winners in ***3-Dimensional Illustrators Awards Annual II****, demonstrate the high standard of excellence and professionalism of 3-D Illustrators, art directors, photographers and animators. Dimensional Illustrators, Inc. would like to thank the judges for their superb selections and wishes them continued success in all their creative endeavors.*

Margaret Cusack

Margaret Cusack is a nationally known 3-Dimensional Illustrator. She has worked as an Art Director, Set Designer and Graphic Designer. Since 1972, Margaret has concentrated her creative energies on fabric collage, samplers and soft sculpture. Her illustrations have enhanced the covers of the nation's leading magazines.

Margaret is a graduate of the Pratt Institute and is a member of the Graphic Artists Guild. In 1989 and 1990, she organized the Dimensional Illustrators Event. This annual portfolio showcase features the nation's top 3-D illustrators. She is a lecturer and served as the panel moderator of the Grafix '90 show in New York entitled, ***The Business of 3-Dimensional Illustration****.*

Her awards include an Emmy in 1971 for set design, the Pratt Institute Alumni Achievement Award, Society of Illustrators Awards, Gold and Silver Awards in the Dimensional Illustrators Awards Show and a 1975 Andy Award.

Mike Jaycock

Mike Jaycock is Vice President, Creative, with the Canadian agency, Kelley Advertising, Inc. An experienced practitioner, Mike has had a varied and illustrious career including time as Broadcaster, Media Manager, Broadcast Producer, Account Supervisor and Vice President. Mike's colleagues agree that his enthusiasm and bon vivant personality are ideally suited for the communications industry.

He believes that,"Creative advertising is the reward that comes from hard work, clear thinking, a little courage and the never-ending search for new insights. When the client and the agency share this view, the relationship is bound to be successful."

Mike maintains an active pace in community work with business, education and public service boards. The awards and honors afforded him have included Honorary President of the Ontario Business Education Association, Canadian Advertising and Sales Association Advertising Person of the Year and a National Award from the Canadian Co-operative Career Education Association of Canada. Recently, he received the Premier's Award (Ontario) for service to business and education.

Ajin Noda

Ajin Noda is a self-taught paper sculptor. His uniquely creative designs have contributed to Japan's acceptance of paper sculpture as a legitimate illustration medium.

In 1981, he was awarded the 27th Bunshun Manga Award, Japan's most prestigious prize for excellence in illustration. Two years later, he left his native country to pursue a new career in America. Ajin has overcome language, commercial and artistic barriers to re-establish himself as one of America's leading paper sculptors.

Today, his portfolio includes an international array of clients. His work has been exhibited at the National Portrait Gallery of the Smithsonian Institute, in Washington D.C. and the Permanent Exhibition at the Mobil Oil Art Collection in Fairfax, Virginia.

Ajin has received awards from the Society of Illustrators, The Art Directors Club of New York City, Educational Press Association of America and the Dimensional Illustrators Awards Show.

B. Martin Pedersen

B. Martin Pedersen is the Publisher and Creative Director of Graphis Magazine. His career encompassed both advertising and corporate design. In 1966, he was made Corporate Design Director of American Airlines, and two years later he established his own firm, Pedersen Design, Inc. In 1978, he was a major partner in the design firm of Johnson Pedersen Hinrichs & Shakery. Mr. Pedersen purchased Graphis Press, an international publishing firm that produces Graphis Magazine, books and annuals for the communications industry.

A former university instructor, he is a frequent lecturer at design conferences and seminars. He is presently on the Board of Directors for the Type Directors Club and has served on the Board of Directors for The New York Art Directors Club. Mr. Pedersen is a member of the Society of Illustrators and Alliance Graphique International.

Mr. Pedersen has received more than 300 major awards for his creative work, including seven Gold and three Silver Awards from The Art Directors Club of New York. Also, he has won awards from the American Institute of Graphic Artists, the Society of Publication Designers, the Society of Illustrators and the Type Directors Club of New York. His work has been exhibited in the Charlottenberg Museum, Copenhagen, Herning Kunst Museum, Herning Denmark, the Klostertorv 9 Gallery for Design and Architecture, Aarhus Denmark and the Whitney Museum, New York.

Ross Sutherland

Ross Sutherland is Senior Vice President, Creative Director with Ogilvy & Mather New York. He was born in Auckland, New Zealand. In 1971, after a brief fine art career, Ross became a Junior Art Director with Ogilvy & Mather New Zealand.

During his career he has worked in New Zealand, Thailand, Singapore, Hong Kong and Kenya. In 1981, Ross and fellow New Zealander John Doig became partners in a local Hong Kong agency. Later, Ross returned to Ogilvy & Mather to start the Meridian Group of agencies. In 1985, he returned to New York where he currently resides with his wife and thirteen-year-old son.

Ross has witnessed many advertising changes during his twenty year career with Ogilvy & Mather. His international experience brings a unique cultural perspective to all his creative endeavors.

Will Vinton

Will Vinton is the Chief Executive Officer of Will Vinton Productions in Portland, Oregon. He is the creator of the stop motion animation process known as Claymation.® In 1975, he was awarded an Academy Award for best animated short film for ***Closed Mondays****, co-created with Bob Gardiner. He has received two Emmy Awards for* ***A Claymation Christmas Celebration*** *and a combined live action/Claymation sequence on the network series,* ***Moonlighting****. Mr. Vinton is credited with the first all-Claymation feature film entitled,* ***The Adventures of Mark Twain****.*

In 1986, the company received worldwide accolades for the most memorable commercial of all time, ***The California Raisins****.™ This was followed by a theatrical commercial featuring a Claymation Michael Jackson.*

Recently, he directed a Ralston Purina TV commercial entitled, ***Turtle Song****, which marked the Claymation debut of the Teenage Mutant Ninja Turtles.® Mr. Vinton's distinct style received international recognition when the Annecy and Hiroshima festivals honored him with major retrospectives of his work. International clients include Beecham Cough Caps and Typhoo QT for the UK, Baume Kamol for France and Aquarious Soft Drinks and Takeda C-1000 for Japan.*

Dimensional illustrators working in mixed media fuse unrelated objects into positive conceptual images. The most fundamental elements are combined to create intrinsically appealing models and props. Their creative freedom places them into a distinctive class of modelmakers. The aesthetic imagery created from found objects, sculptural assemblage and modelmaking requires a complete mastery of 3-Dimensional design techniques. Coupled with creative art direction and photography, the printed piece offers solutions that have a greater impact on the viewer.

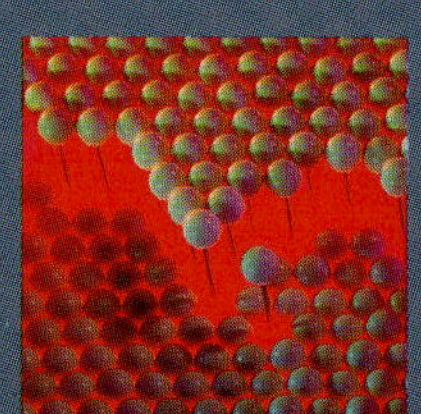

Ethnic Origins Of The U.S.

3-D Illustrator: Joanne Hoffman
Art Director: Joanne Hoffman
Photographer: Seymour Mednick
Agency: Sonder-Levitt
Publisher: Balch Institute
Client: Balch Institute
Category: Editorial Illustration

White Horse

3-D Illustrator: Mark Yurkiw Ltd.
Art Director: Mark Tutssel
Photographer: David Zimmerman
Agency: Leo Burnett/London
Client: Arthur Bell Distillers-White Horse Whiskey
Category: Billboard

Fisherman

3-D Illustrator: Lee & Mary Sievers
Art Director: Lee Sievers
Photographer: Tom Nelson
Client: Meadowcreek Gallery
Category: Unpublished

MIXED MEDIA

West

3-D Illustrator: Fred Otnes
Art Director: Howard Paine
Client: Artists Associates/National Geographic
Category: Consumer Magazine Full Page

Victoriana Calendar
Paper Ephemera from the John Grossman
Collection of Antique Images Circa 1820-1920

3-D Illustrator: Cynthia Hart
Art Director: Paul Hanson
Photographer: Nebil Ozgen
Agency: Cynthia Hart Designer, NYC
Publisher: Workman Publishing
Client: Peter Workman
Category: Complete Calendar

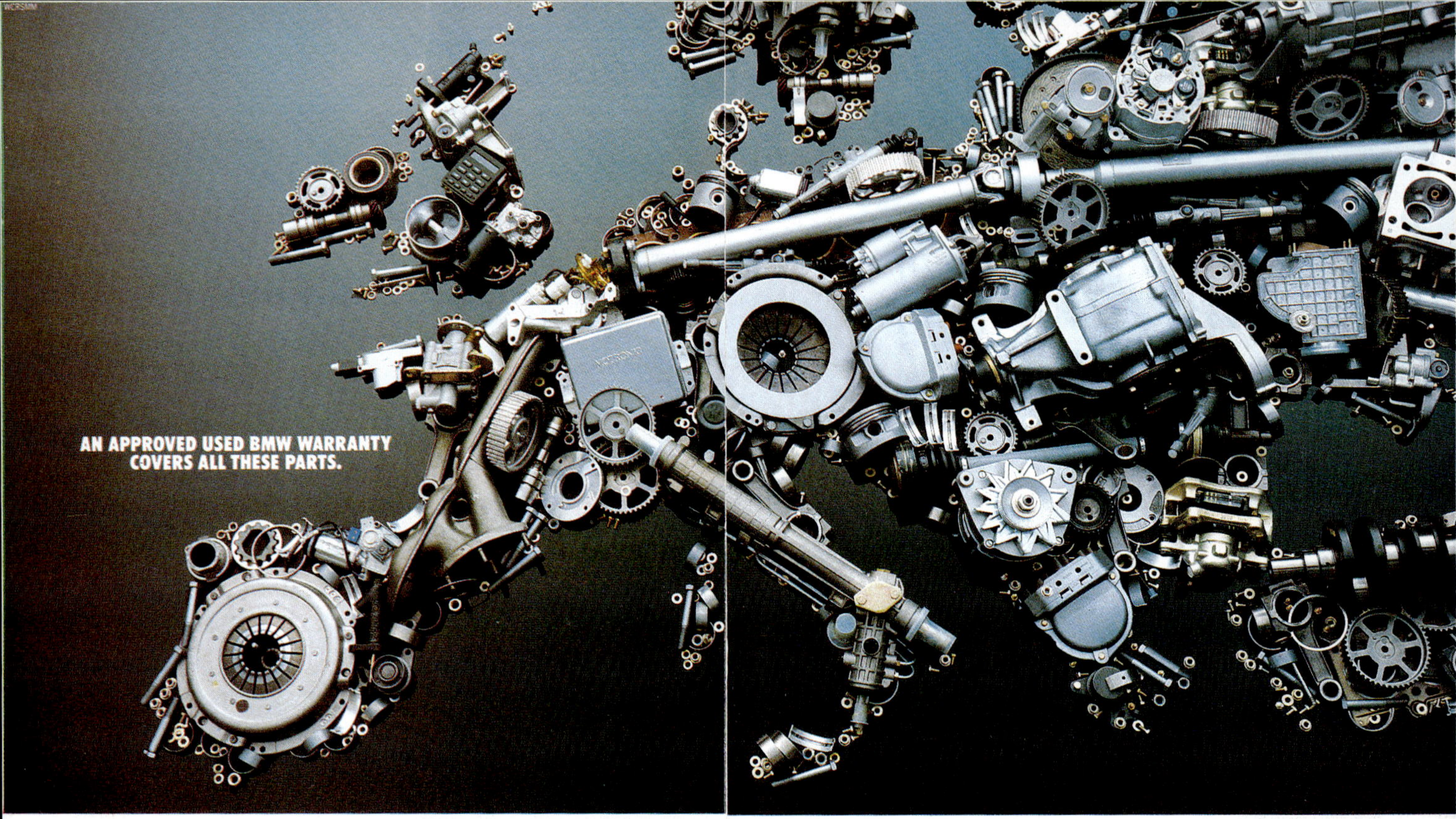

Wherever you wend your way in Europe, you'll be covered by the Approved Used BMW Warranty.

And not simply for the replacement of parts.

It also guarantees that most welcome of sights.

An emergency breakdown van appearing over the brow of the Sierra Nevada. Pronto.

If the problem can't be fixed there and then, your car will be taken to the nearest authorised BMW dealer.

Of course, there's always a slim chance their man in Avignon might not have the right 'alternateur' in stock.

Or their man in Wiesbaden might not have the correct 'Wasserpumpe' to hand.

Whatever the part or part of Europe, BMW's Emergency Service can find what's needed and pay for it to be delivered.

Should the repair take more than four hours, you're covered for the cost of a hired car for up to two weeks.

And if it represents more than a day's work, your car will be repatriated to the UK.

You and your family receive similar care and attention.

Should anyone fall ill, their medical costs are covered until they're back on the road again, in perfect working order.

Your financial welfare is also taken care of.

Every single Approved Used car receives an extensive multi-point check to ensure that it runs just as economically and efficiently as it did when it was new.

And there's the added security of BMW Finance, available on every Approved Used car.

After all, holidays are all about relaxing.

And relax you can behind the wheel of an Approved Used BMW. Anywhere in Europe.

To: BMW Information Service, PO Box 46, Hounslow, Middlesex TW4 6NF. Tel: 01-897 6665.
Please send me a BMW Approved Used Car Information File and the name of my local dealer.

(Mr, Mrs, Miss, etc.) Initial Surname Address AM/1/C/1

Town County

Post Code Telephone

Present Car Year of reg. Age if under 18

Approved Used Cars

FOR FULL WRITTEN DETAILS OF THE TERMS, CONDITIONS AND EXCLUSIONS OF THE BMW APPROVED USED CAR WARRANTY CONTACT YOUR NEAREST AUTHORISED BMW DEALER. THE MANIFOLD SHOWN IS ONLY COVERED WHEN AN APPROVED USED CAR IS SOLD UNDER A BMW NEW CAR EXTENSION POLICY.

BMW Map Of Europe

3-D Illustrator: Malcolm Fowler/Nancy Fouts
Art Director: Andy Anadeo
Photographer: Graham Ford
Agency: WCRS London
Client: BMW
Category: Consumer Magazine Spread

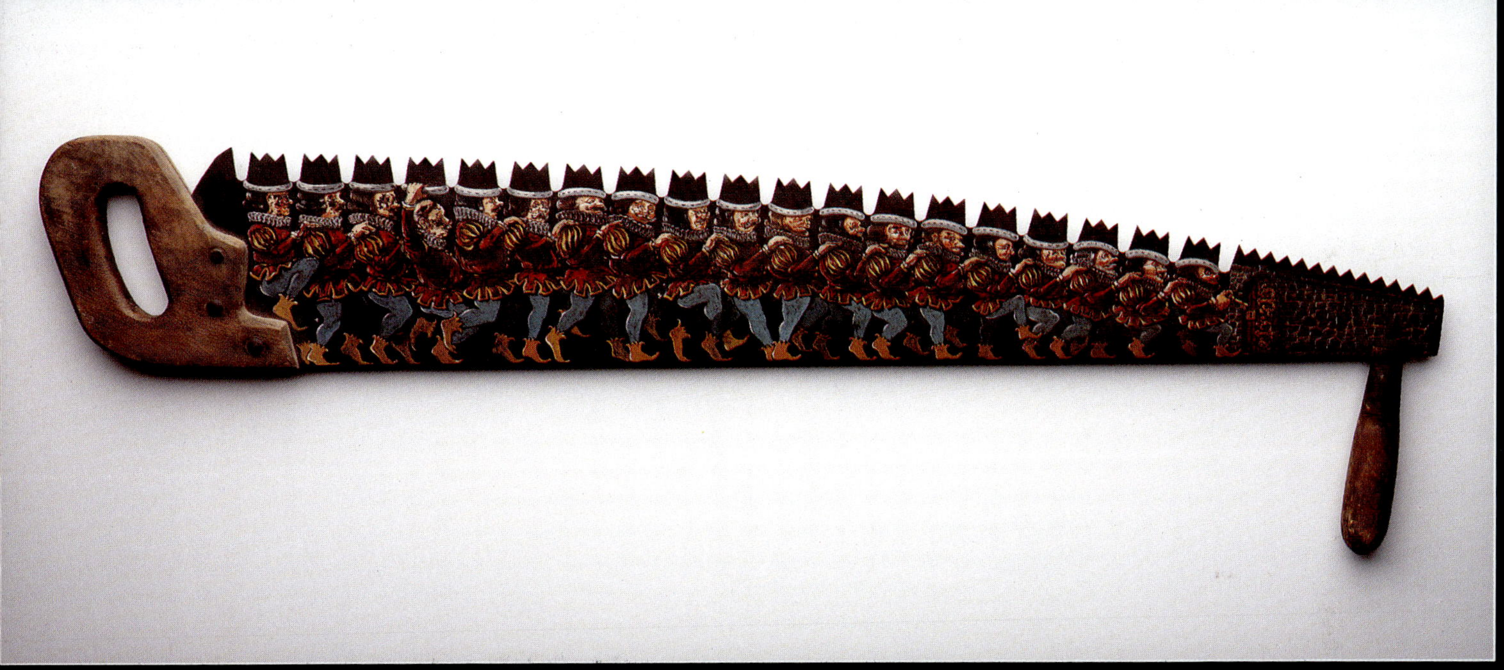

King Size Saw

3-D Illustrator: Malcolm Fowler
Art Director: Malcolm Fowler
Photographer: Nancy Fouts
Agency: Shirt Sleeve Studio London
Client: Shirt Sleeve Studio London
Category: Unpublished

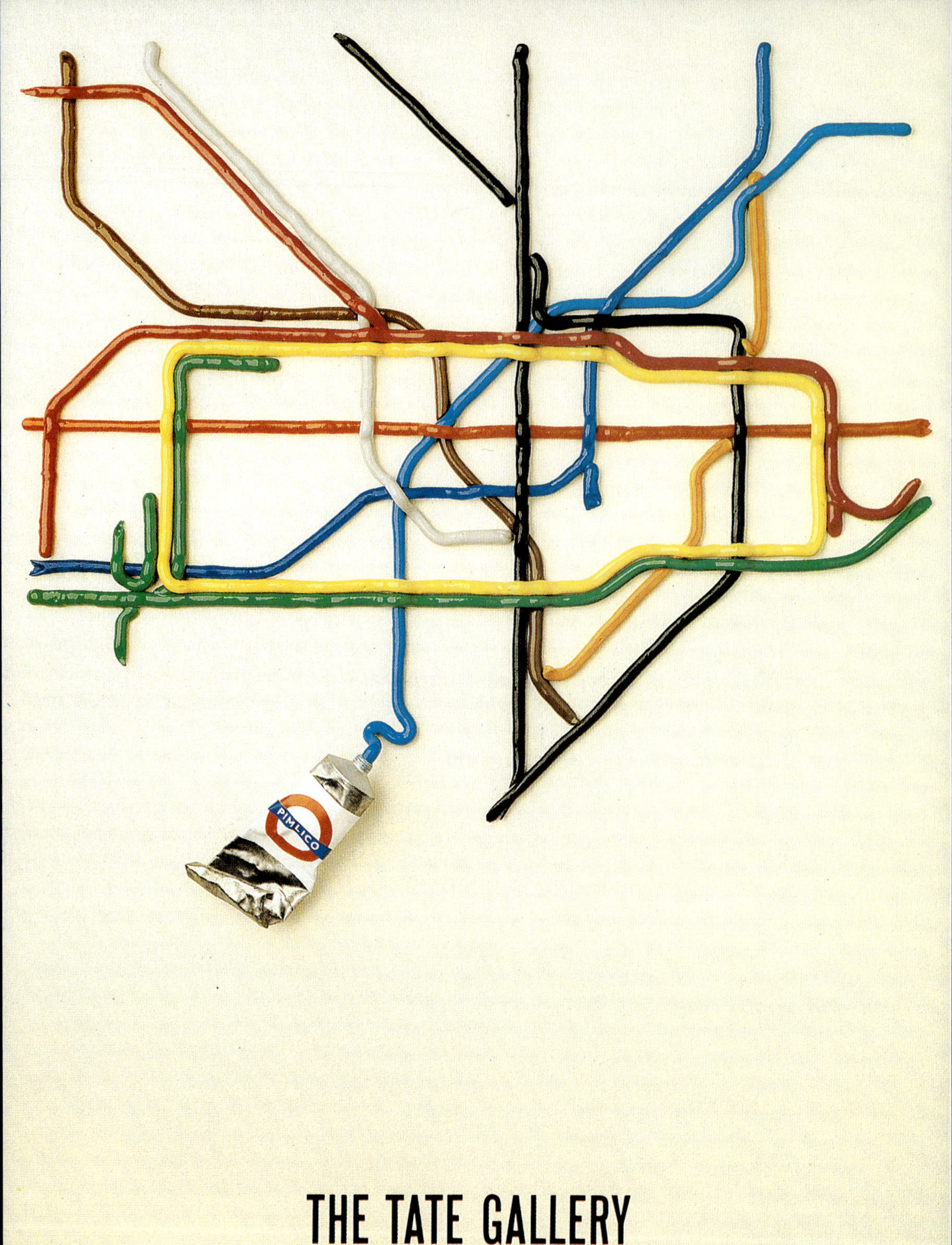

Tate By Tube Poster

3-D Illustrator: Malcolm Fowler/Mark Plenderleith
Art Director: David Hughes/David Booth
Photographer: John Hammond
Agency: Shirt Sleeve Studios London
Publisher: Fine White Line
Client: London Transport Tube

Subway Sardines

3-D Illustrator: Nick Koudis
CD/Copywriter: John Florio
Art Director: Keith Druckenmiller/Al Gobea
Photographer: Nick Koudis
Agency: Corbett Florio Lord, Inc.

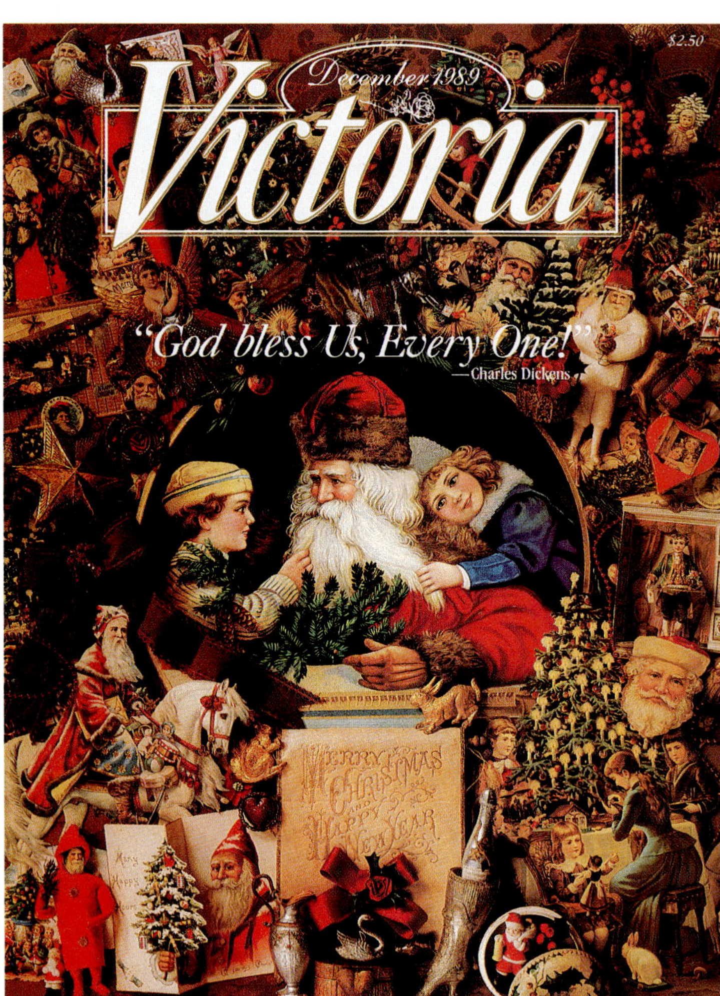

Victoria Cover—December
Paper Ephemera from the John Grossman Collection of Antique Images Circa 1820-1920

3-D Illustrator: Cynthia Hart
Art Director: Bryan E. McCay
Photographer: Steven Tex
Agency: Cynthia Hart Designer, NYC
Publisher: Hearst Magazines/Victoria Magazine
Client: Nancy Lindemeyer, Editor
Category: Consumer Magazine Cover

Moonshadow

3-D Illustrator: Joe LaMantia
Art Director: Jon Tribble
Photographer: David Dudine
Agency: LaMantia Studio
Publisher: Indiana University
Client: Indiana University
Category: Consumer Magazine Cover

DBMS: Beyond Plain Vanilla

3-D Illustrator: Kathy Jeffers
Art Director: Ken Surabian
Photographer: Walter Wick
Publisher: Datamation/Cahners Publishing
Category: Business Magazine Cover

Rom Disc

3-D Illustrator: Bob Saint John
Art Director: Linda Sweeney
Photographer: Bob Saint John
Publisher: CD-Rom
Client: CD-Rom Magazine
Category: Consumer Magazine Cover

Robotics: Boon or Bust In the Lab

3-D Illustrator: James Nazz
Art Director: Kathleen Cuddihy
Photographer: James Nazz
Publisher: Medical Economics Company
Client: MLO
Category: Business Magazine Cover

A-Train

3-D Illustrator: Joe LaMantia
Art Director: Carol Bucheri
Photographer: David Dudine
Agency: LaMantia Studio
Publisher: Phi Delta Kappa, Inc.
Client: Phi Delta Kappan
Category: Business Magazine Spread

A CAHNERS PUBLICATION
AUGUST 15, 1989
EMERGENCY MEDICINE
ACUTE MEDICINE FOR THE PRIMARY CARE PHYSICIAN
STROKE: BUT WHICH KIND?
The Diagnostic Psychiatric Interview
Oral Intubation in Adults
Lyme Heart Block
ANNUAL LIST OF POISON CONTROL CENTERS

Stroke: But Which Kind?

3-D Illustrator: Jane Stein/Tina Chaden
Art Director: Lois Erlacher
Photographer: David Arky
Publisher: Cahners Publishing Company
Client: Emergency Medicine Magazine
Category: Business Magazine Cover

Dairyland

3-D Illustrator: Joe LaMantia
Art Director: Kim McKinney
Photographer: David Dudine
Agency: LaMantia Studio
Publisher: Indiana University/Bloomington
Client: Indiana Review
Category: Consumer Magazine Cover

How Much Have Your Colleagues Raised Their Fees?

3-D Illustrator: Joan Steiner
Art Director: William Kuhn
Photographer: Stephen E. Munz
Publisher: Medical Economics Company
Client: Medical Economics Company For Surgeons
Category: Business Magazine Cover

How Much Have Your Colleagues Raised Their Fees?

3-D Illustrator: Joan Steiner
Art Director: William Kuhn
Photographer: Stephen E. Munz
Publisher: Medical Economics Company
Client: Medical Economics For Surgeons
Category: Business Magazine Spread

HOW MUCH HAVE YOUR COLLEAGUES RAISED THEIR FEES?

Quite sharply, in many cases. But overall, our 1989 survey shows, the increases were more selective than in recent years.

By Mark Crane SENIOR EDITOR

The debate about relative value scales and other forms of cost containment has focused increasingly on fees for big-ticket surgical procedures. For most of this decade, the implicit message by the health-care bureaucracy has been clear: Put a lid on your charges or we'll do it for you.

Despite that threat, the physicians' services component of the Consumer Price Index was projected to rise by 9.0 percent in 1989, making this the ninth year in a row that medical fee increases have outdistanced the overall rise in the CPI. That also promises to be the largest increase since 1981, and would be 1.5 percentage points ahead of last year.

THIS ARTICLE is copyright © 1989 and published by Medical Economics Company Inc. at Oradell, N.J. 07649. All rights reserved. It may not be reproduced, quoted, or paraphrased in whole or in part in any manner whatsoever without the prior written permission of the copyright owner.

One bit of encouraging news is that the gap between the medical profession's fee hike and the overall inflation rate is narrowing somewhat. But that's only because the projected CPI increase of 5.7 percent is also the highest in years.

Other good news is that fee hikes in the six fields we surveyed for this report (general, orthopedic, plastic, thoracic, cardiovascular, and neurosurgery) were more modest than in many other fields, according to our latest Continuing Survey. Fees for a selection of operations rose by an average of 6.5 percent. In 1988, fees for the same procedures shot up by an average of 10 percent, following the modest rise of 2.5 percent the year before.

Moreover, of the 38 procedures most often performed by these specialists, seven showed no statistically significant increase from the spring of 1988 to the spring of 1989 (when our surveys were conducted), and eight others had only nominal hikes of 3 percent or less. The remaining 23 procedures increased by an average of 10 percent.

Often, surgeons raise only a few fees at a time. For example, orthopedists boosted their median fees for seven procedures by an average of 11.4 percent since the 1988 survey. But these M.D.s were making up for

20 OCTOBER 1989

Nielson Review of Supermarket Trends

3-D Illustrator: Gary Eldridge
Corp.Art Director: Jean DeVito
Art Director: Joe Kantorski
Photographer: Phil Schaafsma
Publisher: The Progressive Grocer
Category: Business Magazine Cover

Why Some Colleagues' Fees Are Sky-High

3-D Illustrator: Joan Steiner
Art Director: Roger Dowd/Ann Weber
Photographer: Walter Wick
Publisher: Medical Economics Company
Client: Medical Economics Company
Category: Business Magazine Cover

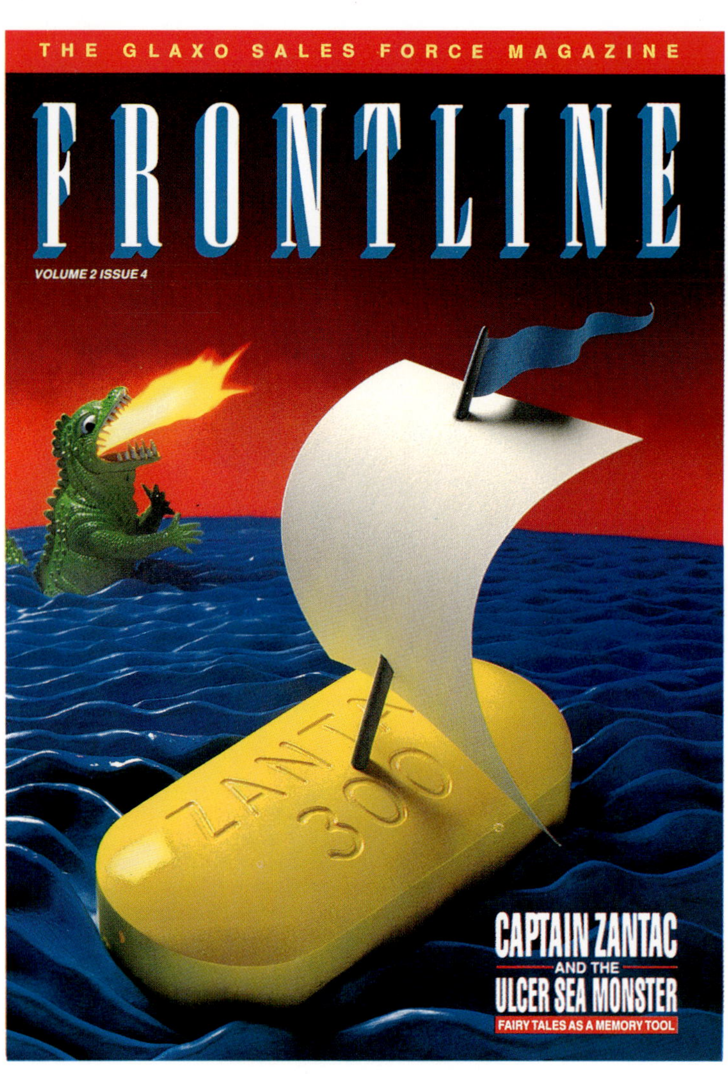

Captain Zantac

3-D Illustrator: Douglass Grimmett
Art Director: Martha Lewis Bell
Photographer: Chuck Carlton
Agency: FGI
Client: Glaxo
Category: Business Magazine Cover

Purchasing Helped Xerox Win the Baldrige

3-D Illustrator: Gary Eldridge
Art Director: Allen Rantz
Photographer: Corrie Knoll/Labakk Studio
Publisher: Electronics Purchasing
Category: Business Magazine Spread

Too Close To Home

3-D Illustrator: Gary Eldridge
Art Director: Shauna Wolf Narciso
Photographer: Phil Schaafsma
Publisher: Pacific Northwest Media, Inc.
Category: Consumer Magazine Full Page

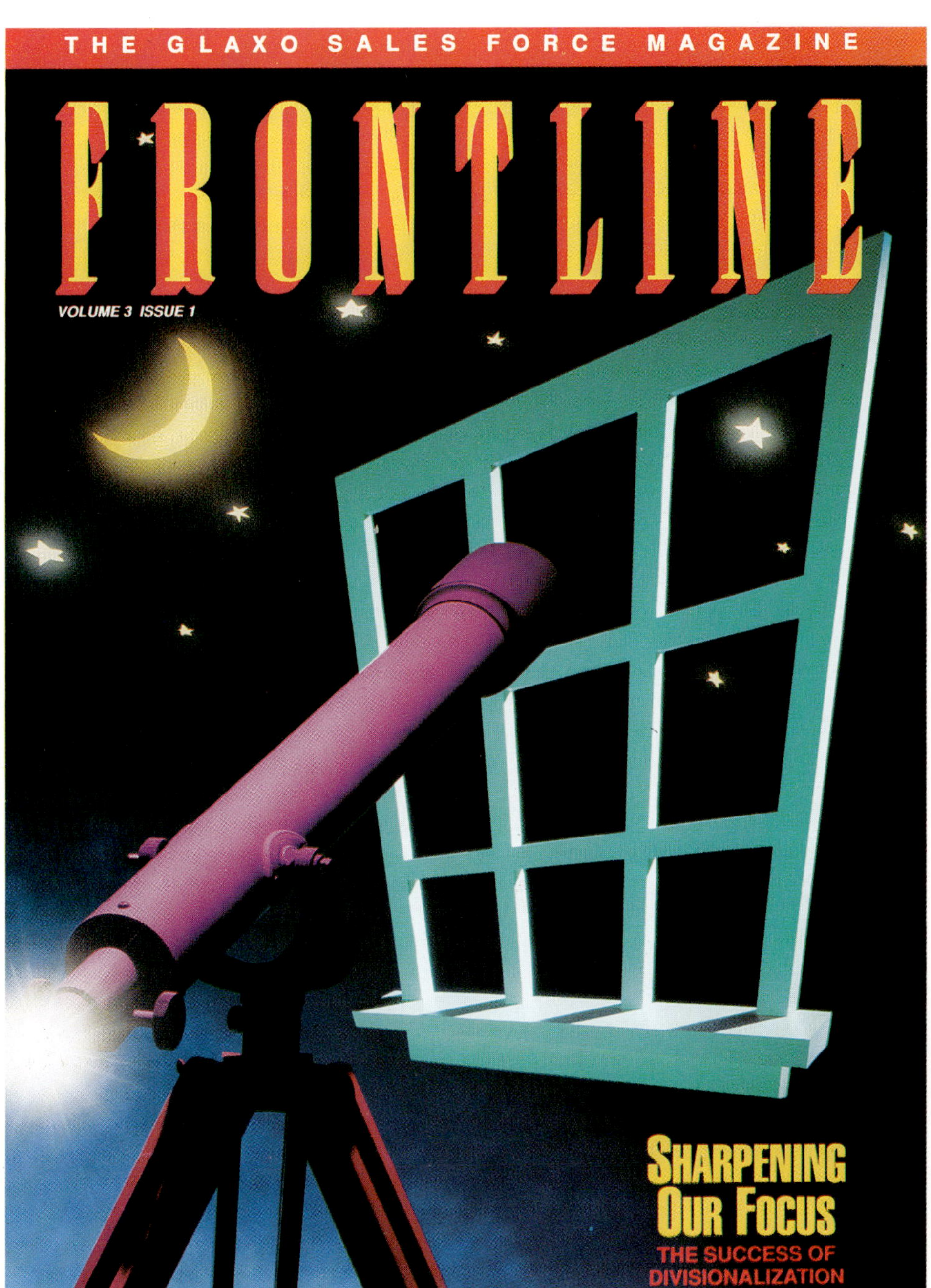

Sharpening Our Focus

3-D Illustrator: Douglass Grimmett
Art Director: Martha Lewis Bell
Photographer: Chuck Carlton
Agency: FGI
Client: Glaxo
Category: Business Magazine Cover

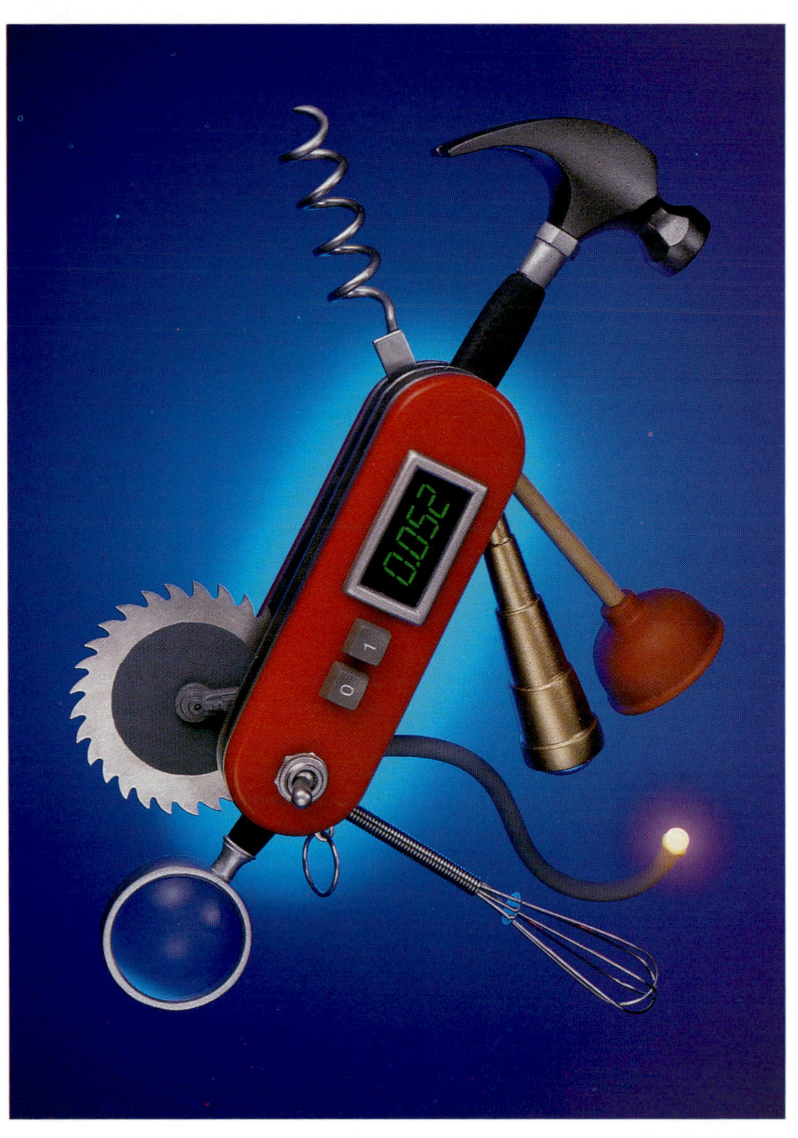

What Kind Of Tool Am I?

3-D Illustrator: Kathy Jeffers
Art Director: Ken Surabian
Photographer: Chuck Carlton
Publisher: Datamation Magazine
Category: Business Magazine Cover

My Semi-Tough Return To Playing Golf

3-D Illustrator: Tak Murakami
Art Director: Nick DiDio
Photographer: Tak Murakami
Publisher: Golf Digest Magazine
Client: Golf Digest Magazine
Category: Editorial Illustration

HUMOR

MY SEMI-TOUGH RETURN TO PLAYING GOLF

His game went south, but after 26 years in New York the author moved to Florida and found it again

BY DAN JENKINS

It is no big secret that the game of golf requires grave concentration to be played decently, so let me say right off that it is not altogether to your advantage while you're standing over a 5-iron shot to be thinking: "I've got to remember to get some Freon in the Toyota."

Freon shots are my life these days. They are the kind of shots, which, after you hit four inches behind them, float lazily into a lagoon, forest or marsh. Freon shots are what happen to you all too often when you take up the game again after a 10-year layoff.

I call them Freon shots but they have other names, such as:

1. The Phillips screwdriver shot, as in, "I know there used to be one in that drawer."

2. The frozen dinner shot, as in, "I'm sure we're out of creamed chipped beef and chicken pot pie."

3. The electrician shot, as in, "It's usually the circuit breaker but this time it's not."

4. The VCR shot, as in, "You'd think the manual would tell you how to set the damn timer."

And most familiarly:

5. The no-count, low-life, rotten summitch.

Actually, the Freon shot comes later. When you take up the game again after a long absence, there is a more urgent problem.

The first thing you discover is that

Spotting Trends

3-D Illustrator: Douglass Grimmett
Art Director: Carol Erger Fass
Photographer: Michael Kellough
Agency: Grimmett Corporation
Publisher: Adweek
Client: Adweek
Category: Business Magazine Cover

Metal Lady

3-D Illustrator: Peter Botsis
Art Director: Peter Botsis
Photographer: Sue Weller
Category: Business Magazine Cover

Telephone & Filing Resources

3-D Illustrator: Rick Schneider
Art Director: David Beverage
Publisher: Springhouse Corporation
Client: Office Systems Magazine
Category: Business Magazine Cover

Global Village

3-D Illustrator: Doug Grimmett
Art Director: Wally Lawrence
Photographer: Chuck Carlton
Publisher: Adweek Magazine
Client: Adweek Magazine
Category: Business Magazine Spread

Getting It Write

3-D Illustrator: Elizabeth Traynor
Art Director: Mike Melia/Mark Steingruber
Photographer: David Guggenheim
Agency: Melia Design Group
Publisher: Agnes Scott Magazine
Client: Agnes Scott Magazine
Category: Business Magazine Full Page

Reflections On Academic Life

3-D Illustrator: Lindy Burnett
Art Director: Mike Melia
Photographer: David Guggenheim
Agency: Melia Design Group
Publisher: Agnes Scott Magazine
Client: Agnes Scott Magazine
Category: Business Magazine Full Page

Flying Carpet

3-D Illustrator: Chuck Carlton
Art Director: Walter McCord/Julia Comer
Photographer: Chuck Carlton
Agency: Envision Design
Publisher: Louisville Magazine
Client: Francis Lee Jasper
Category: Consumer Magazine Full Page

Maxi-Swatch

3-D Illustrator: Chuck Carlton/David P. Reaves III
Art Director: Julie Koch-Beinke
Photographer: Chuck Carlton
Agency: Alternatives, Inc.
Client: Swatch Watch USA
Category: Advertising Direct Mail Brochure

Will You Know When It's True Love?

Years of dating have made it difficult for some of us to recognize the real thing when it comes along. There's no single indication but, rather, a host of factors merrily at play.

66 New Woman • October 1989

Will You Know When It's True Love?

3-D Illustrator: Frank Maraschiello
Art Director: Catherine Caldwell
Photographer: Judd Pilossof
Publisher: Murdoch Publishers
Client: New Women Magazine
Category: Editorial Illustration

Rock Music: Can It Hurt Your Child?

3-D Illustrator: Frank Maraschiello
Art Director: Amy Gottlieb
Photographer: Judd Pilossof
Publisher: Rodale Press
Client: Children Magazine
Category: Editorial Illustration

ROCK MUSIC

CAN IT HURT YOUR CHILD?

BY SHARON FAELTEN

The classic rock-and-roll hit "Louie Louie" is about:

a. summer love
b. a lost cat
c. torrid, lewd sexual acts
d. any or all of the above

If you answered "d," you know that the lyrics to this greatest hit of The Kingsmen are in gibberish, a native dialect of rock music. But when "Louie Louie" was first released in 1962, many radio stations refused to play it. Critics were convinced that the words were obscene and would corrupt young listeners.

Fast forward to the Eighties. The brouhaha over "Louie Louie" pales beside current rock-and-roll controversies. The rumors that Ozzy Osborne, the dean of heavy metal, bit the head off a live bat during a stage performance a couple of years ago make antics like Elvis' gyroscopic hip-wriggling look tame by comparison. (Reportedly, Osborne says he thought the bat was a plastic toy tossed on stage by a fan.) News stories of teens who commit Satanic ritual killings—or kill themselves—under the alleged influence of popular bands such as AC/DC mystify, shock and puzzle parents who never came closer to acting out a rock-and-roll fantasy than playing air guitar in front of a mirror to favorite Beatles' songs.

KIDS GRADUATE
FROM SESAME STREET
TO MTV. ROCK IS
THE SOUNDTRACK OF LIFE

ARE YOU TUNED IN?

AUGUST 1988 • 69

Disappearing Through The Skylight

3-D Illustrator: Cathy Saksa
Art Director: Neil Stewart
Publisher: Viking/Penguin
Category: Book Cover

Point Of View

3-D Illustrator: Joan Hall
Art Director: Marta Ruliffson
Photographer: David Lawrence
Agency: MKR Design
Client: Scholastic
Category: Software Cover

Letters From A Soviet Prison Camp

3-D Illustrator: Gary Eldridge
Art Director: Dwight Baker
Photographer: Phil Schaafsma
Publisher: Baker Book House
Category: Book Cover

Fall Catalogue Cover

3-D Illustrator: Joan Steiner
Art Director: Emil Micha
Photographer: Walter Wick
Publisher: Prentice Hall Press
Client: Prentice Hall Press
Category: Catalogue Cover

Natural Beauty Begins With Caring

3-D Illustrator: Kimberly Spencer
Art Director: Kimberly Spencer
Photographer: Andy Terzes
Agency: Salon Enterprises
Copy: Linda Christy
Publisher: Various Art Programs
Client: Panopoulos Salons
Category: Consumer Magazine Less Than Full Page

Robot Hand

3-D Illustrator: Joan Kritchman/Knuteson
Art Director: Wendy Hinrichs Patti
Photographer: Tom Barnes Studio
Agency: Design Partners
Client: Master Appliance Corporation
Category: Advertising Business Direct Mail Brochure

Integrated Marketing Services

3-D Illustrator: Douglass Grimmett
Art Director: Douglass Grimmett
Photographer: Chuck Carlton
Agency: FGI
Client: FGI
Category: Advertising Direct Mail Brochure

A World Of Drug Information

3-D Illustrator: Kathleen Ziegler
Art Director: Tina Cipriani/Ira Grunther
Photographer: Kathleen Ziegler
Agency: Grunther Associates
Publisher: Excerpta Medica
Client: Excerpta Medica
Category: Business Magazine Full Page

The Island

3-D Illustrator: Achim Kiel
Art Director: Achim Kiel
Photographer: Uwe Brandes
Agency: Pencil Corporate Art
Publisher: Octant Kunststoffdruck
Client: WWF Germany
Category: Consumer Magazine Cover

Bird With Rose

3-D Illustrator: Fred Otnes
Art Director: Herman Vanderberg
Agency: Lowe Marschalk
Client: Artists Associates
Category: Consumer Magazine Full Page

The Preminger Art Collection

3-D Illustrator: Achim Kiel
Art Director: Achim Kiel
Photographer: Ute Karen Walter/Uwe Brandes
Agency: Pencil Corporate Art
Publisher: Pencil Corporate Art & Plumhoff & Dueker
Client: Heinrich Dueker & Carsten Vollmers
Category: Advertising Business Direct Mail Brochure

Dollar Sign

3-D Illustrator: Bob Emmott
Art Director: Jake Smith
Photographer: Emmott Photography, Inc.
Client: Springhouse Corporation
Category: Editorial Illustration

Sr. PGA Tour 40+

3-D Illustrator: James Nazz
Art Director: Debbie Chute
Photographer: James Nazz
Publisher: Golf Digest
Client: Golf Digest
Category: Consumer Magazine Spread

Cast Hand

3-D Illustrator: Fred Otnes
Art Director: Fred Otnes
Client: Artists Associates
Category: Consumer Magazine Full Page

State Of Corrosion

3-D Illustrator: The Object Works
Art Director: Frank Palmer
Photographer: Walt Seng
Agency: Della Femina McNamee WCRS
Client: Bayer USA, Inc.
Category: Business Magazine Spread

Only the best bridge coatings can survive this state of corrosion.

West Banana River Bridge

The three-coat urethane system was outstanding in a three-year test at the West Banana River Bridge.

In the state of Florida, the effects of salt spray, wind, heat and humidity combine to challenge even the most durable of high-performance coating systems.

Near Cocoa Beach at the West Banana River Bridge, a new three-coat urethane system not only survived, but exhibited less than 0.5 percent rusting at the end of a three-year test by the Florida Department of Transportation. This exceptional performance is the result of the system's special combination of properties:

- Wide recoat window. The recoat time for the primer can be from two hours to three months. Or, for the intermediate and top coats, from four hours to years.
- Cold curing at temperatures as low as 0°F.
- Excellent adhesion. The system exhibits tenacious inter-coat adhesion and superb edge-covering capabilities.
- Outstanding corrosion resistance to the elements and environmental pollutants with excellent color and gloss retention.
- Meets the 3.5 lb./gal. (420g/l) VOC requirement.

This all-polyurethane bridge coating system is based on raw materials and technology from Mobay—the nation's leading supplier of polyurethanes to paint and coatings manufacturers. The system starts with a zinc-rich primer based on Desmodur E-21 polyisocyanate. With intermediate and top coats based on Desmophen A-160 acrylic polyol and Desmodur N aliphatic polyisocyanate.

For detailed information on the three-coat system and the West Banana River Bridge test, Mobay Corporation has put together a comprehensive four-color brochure. Just circle our reader service number to receive a copy. Or, contact Jack Bracco at 412 777-2876. Mobay Corporation, Coatings Division, Mobay Road, Pittsburgh, PA 15205-9741.

Update

Mobay

A Bayer USA INC. COMPANY

1990 Calendar

3-D Illustrator: Jerry Pavey
Art Director: Jerry Pavey
Photographer: Tom Radcliffe/William McCaw
Agency: Jerry Pavey Design & Illustration
Publisher: S&S Graphics, Inc.
Client: S.D. Warren Paper Co./S&S Graphics, Inc.
Category: Complete Calendar

The Garden City Gardener

3-D Illustrator: Rob Browne
Art Director: Rob Browne
Category: Editorial Illustration

July

3-D Illustrator: Larry Mikec
Art Director: Larry Mikec
Photographer: Allen Knox Photographers
Agency: Art Factory
Client: Art Factory
Category: Calendar Full Page

George Bush

3-D Illustrator: Bob Selby
Art Director: Pete Coffey
Photographer: Dick Benjamin
Publisher: Providence Journal
Client: Providence Journal
Category: Unpublished

Underwater Robot

3-D Illustrator: Douglass Grimmett/Chuck Carlton
Art Director: Douglass Grimmett
Photographer: Chuck Carlton
Publisher: Workman Publishing
Category: Calendar Full Page

Cookbooks For Christmas

3-D Illustrator: Gayle Christensen
Art Director: Gayle Christensen
Photographer: Jon McNally
Agency: Promotion Department
Publisher: Dean Lesher
Client: Food Page
Food Editor: Maggie Crum
Category: Newspaper

Inspector II

3-D Illustrator: Douglass Grimmett/Chuck Carlton
Art Director: Douglass Grimmett
Photographer: Chuck Carlton
Publisher: Workman Publishing
Category: Calendar Full Page

Robowash

3-D Illustrator: Douglass Grimmett/Chuck Carlton
Art Director: Douglass Grimmett
Photographer: Chuck Carlton
Publisher: Workman Publishing
Category: Calendar Full Page

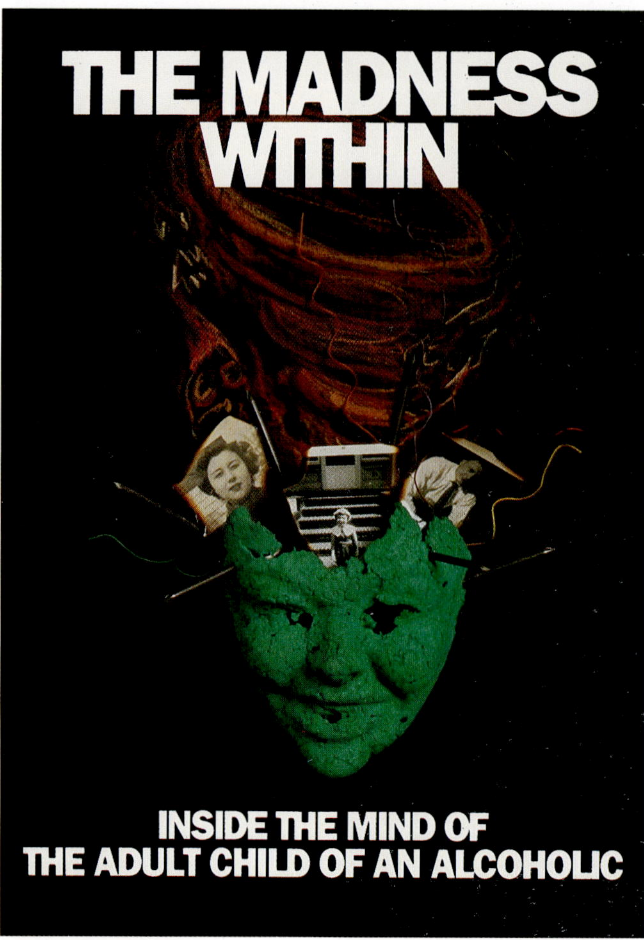

The Madness Within

3-D Illustrator: Marie Corfield
Art Director: Marie Corfield
Photographer: William Wagner
Category: Unpublished

Queen of Heaven—Cruel Side—Goddess of Storms

3-D Illustrator: Ellen Rixford
Art Director: Ellen Rixford
Photographer: Ellen Rixford
Client: Ellen Rixford
Category: Unpublished

Look What You Can Do With Our No. 2

3-D Illustrator: Marie Corfield
Art Director: Marie Corfield
Photographer: William Wagner
Category: Unpublished

Queen of Heaven—Kind Side—Goddess of Dawn

3-D Illustrator: Ellen Rixford
Art Director: Ellen Rixford
Photographer: Ellen Rixford
Client: Ellen Rixford
Category: Unpublished

Swamp Thing

3-D Illustrator: Peter Botsis
Art Director: Peter Botsis
Photographer: Sue Weller
Category: Unpublished

Mount Rushmore

3-D Illustrator: James Sanders
Art Director: Jim Ellingwood
Photographer: Jim Sanders
Agency: ABC
Client: General Hospital
Category: Unpublished

Spirit of Giving

3-D Illustrator: James Sanders
Category: Unpublished

Party Girl Walks The Dogs

3-D Illustrator: Jef Workman
Art Director: Jef Workman
Photographer: Lee Hocker
Agency: Bird In The Hand
Category: Unpublished

Some Little Tragedies Factory

3-D Illustrators: Philipp Gasser/Esther van der Bie
Photographer: Esther van der Bie
Category: Unpublished

Some Little Tragedies Underwater

3-D Illustrator: Philipp Gasser/Esther van der Bie
Photographer: Esther van der Bie
Category: Unpublished

Losing One's Identity In A Nursing Home

3-D Illustrator: Marie Corfield
Art Director: Marie Corfield
Photographer: William Wagner
Category: Unpublished

Chicago Railroad

3-D Illustrator: Fred Otnes
Art Director: Howard Paine
Publisher: National Geographic Magazine
Client: Artists Associates
Category: Self Promotion Flyer

Santa Paws

3-D Illustrator: Lee & Mary Sievers
Art Director: Lee Sievers
Photographer: Tom Nelson
Agency: Ad-Com
Client: Louisville Galleria
Category: Unpublished

Seman's Greetings

3-D Illustrator: The Object Works
Art Director: Richard M. Seman
Photographer: Walt Seng
Agency: The Seman Design Group
Client: The Seman Design Group
Category: Greeting Card

New Year's Cards

3-D Illustrator: Laura Tarrish/Tom Ancona
Art Director: Laura Tarrish/Tom Ancona
Photographer: Tom Ancona
Agency: Laura Tarrish/Tom Ancona
Client: Laura Tarrish/Tom Ancona
Category: Greeting Cards

Tolkien's World

3-D Illustrator: Thomas Frick
Photographer: Thomas Frick
Category: Unpublished
Student: The Maryland Institute College of Art

Addiction

3-D Illustrator: Linda K. Sturm
Photographer: Jellybeans
Category: Unpublished
Student: The College of New Rochelle

Wacky Players

3-D Animator: Jim Downer
Art Director: Bill Jarcho
Director: Bill Jarcho
Studio: Olive Jar Animation
Client: T.J. Lipton Company
Category: TV Commercial

U Know What Time It Is

3-D Animators: Sean Burns, Michael Manning, Tom Winkler, Kevin Lane
Art Director: Bill Jarcho
Director: Bill Jarcho
Studio: Olive Jar Animation
Client: Electra Records/Grand Master Flash
Category: Music Video

Clay sculpture has evolved into a unique illustrative style. Art directors are increasingly selecting clay as an optimum 3-D medium. Soft sculpture clay, plastilina, ceramic clay and clay animation afford the creative director the flexibility to design a myriad of playful yet provocative images. Clay sculpture has an intrinsic ability to evoke a positive response from the viewer and provides a distinctive aesthetic imagery which is difficult to create 2-Dimensionally. Today, clay sculpture has developed a secure niche in the genre of 3-Dimensional Illustration.

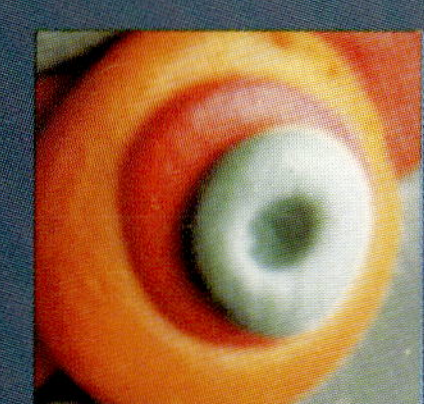

Snail

3-D Illustrator: Malcolm Fowler
Art Director: Carl LeBlondo
Photographer: Nancy Fouts

Tales From The Darkside

Animator: Mark Frizzell
Art Director: Bill Jarcho
Studio: Olive Jar Animation
Client: Tribune Broadcasting
Category: TV Commercial

Spirit Of The Stripes

3-D Illustrator: Jack Graham
Art Director: Kevin Janke
Photographer: Dan Vermillion
Agency: Greymatter Studio

Michael Raisin

Director: Will Vinton
Producer: Marilyn Zornado
Agency: Foote, Cone & Belding
Client: California Raisin Advisory Board
Category: TV Commercial

The Day Dream

3-D Illustrator: Richard McNeel
Art Director: Amy Bass-Wilson
Photographer: William G. Wagner

Facial Proportions

3-D Illustrator: Christopher Bartlett
Art Director: Christopher Bartlett

Stalled

3-D Illustrator: Richard McNeel
Art Director: Laura Baer
Photographer: William G. Wagner
Publisher: Business Week Magazine
Category: Consumer Magazine Cover

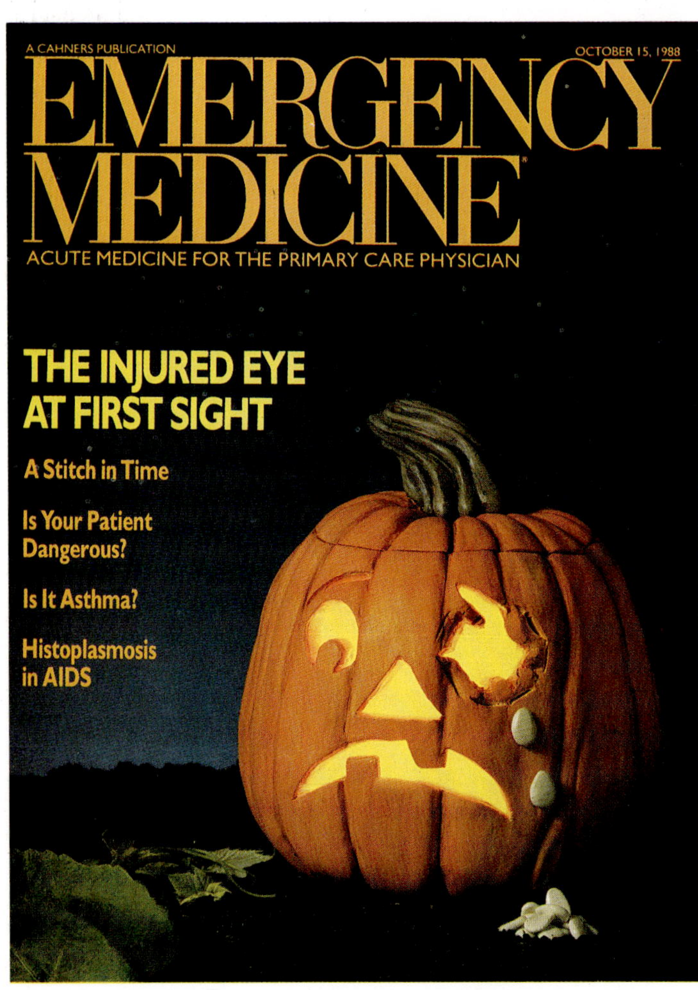

The Injured Eye At First Sight

3-D Illustrator: Christopher Oakley
Art Director: Lois Erlacher
Photographer: Peter Neuman
Publisher: Cahners Publishing Company
Client: Emergency Medicine Magazine
Category: Business Magazine Cover

Cardiogenic Shock

3-D Illustrator: Kathleen Ziegler
Art Director: Ed Rosanio
Photographer: Robert Hakawski
Publisher: Springhouse Corporation
Client: Nursing Magazine
Category: Business Magazine Cover

14 NEW DRUGS: WHAT YOU NEED TO KNOW, p. 57

Action stat! Abdominal stab wound | Administering dopamine safely | Special delivery—transtracheal oxygen | Encouraging a patient with multiple problems

THE WORLD'S LARGEST NURSING JOURNAL | DECEMBER

Nursing89

Protecting MI patients from a deadly complication

CARDIOGENIC SHOCK

...a CE offering, p. 34

Saving The Cardiogenic Shock Patient

3-D Illustrator: Kathleen Ziegler
Art Director: Ed Rosanio
Photographer: Robert Hakawski
Publisher: Springhouse Corporation
Client: Nursing Magazine
Category: Business Magazine Spread

SAVING THE CARDIOGENIC SHOCK PATIENT

Earn CEUs
ANA/AACN-APPROVED

Cardiogenic shock is the Armageddon of heart disease. With a mortality rate approaching 90%, this ominous condition nearly always signals the last days of a failing heart. About 15% to 20% of patients admitted to the hospital with a diagnosis of myocardial infarction (MI) will sustain enough myocardial damage to go into cardiogenic shock. Most of these patients die within 24 hours. Few live more than 4 days.

The earlier this condition is detected and treated, the better the prognosis. That's why you need to be familiar with the signs and symptoms of cardio-

BY ANNA GAWLINSKI, RN, CCRN, MSN
Cardiovascular Clinical Nurse Specialist • UCLA Medical Center
Assistant Professor • UCLA School of Nursing • Los Angeles, California

SCULPTURE BY KATHY ZIEGLER/PHOTOGRAPHY BY ROBERT HAKAWSKI

34 Nursing89, December

Bacchus-The God Of Wine

3-D Illustrator: Kathy Jeffers
Art Director: Hiden Kato
Photographer: Chris Vincent
Publisher: Bacchus Magazine
Category: Consumer Magazine Campaign

B
Bacchus

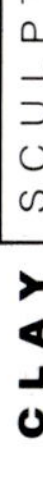

Nursing Income

3-D Illustrator: Joan Steiner/Mary M.Bono
Art Director: Andrea DiBenedetto
Photographer: Ken Schroers
Publisher: Medical Economics Company
Client: RN Magazine
Category: Business Magazine Cover

Alan Greenspan As A Marionette

3-D Illustrator: Ellen Rixford
Art Director: Chel Dong
Photographer: Ellen Rixford
Publisher: Institutional Investor
Client: Institutional Investor
Category: Business Magazine Cover

Deckbuilding

3-D Illustrator: Robert Chatwin
Art Director: David Clubine/Peter Clayton
Photographer: Peter Hogan
Agency: Peter Hogan & Associates
Client: Beaver Lumber
Category: Advertising Consumer Cover

Remember

3-D Illustrator: Douglas Watson
Art Director: Alasdair Chisolm
Photographer: Dougie McBride
Agency: Baillie Marshall Design
Client: Tayside Region Industrial Office
Category: Advertising Business Direct Mail Brochure

Money By Jordan E. Cohn

Charity Wise

The artful giver makes every contribution count

'Tis the season to be generous. Come holiday time, charities are out in full force, expertly tugging at heartstrings and purse strings by mail, phone, doorbell, and workplace. Americans gave close to $94 billion in 1987—almost half, 46.6 percent, going to religion, 14.6 percent to health, 11.6 percent to education, 10.5 percent to human services, and 6.8 percent to arts, culture, and humanities (according to the American Association of Fund-Raising Counsel Trust for Philanthropy). Clearly, to give or not to give is *not* the question, but, rather, how to give wisely. "Sifting through the mass of appeals and requests can be a confusing process," says Tracy Gary, cofounder of the Women's Foundation in San Francisco. "The challenge is to find charities that inspire confidence but at the same time meet social needs."

For most Americans, that means giving to institutions with which they are closely affiliated. Consider Linda Peterson, principal and partner in Peterson Skolnick Dodge, a creative services agency in San Francisco. Peterson's original business partner contracted AIDS; now she and her husband give to a variety of AIDS groups, including the San Francisco AIDS Foundation. A musician and a feminist, she takes care of two causes with one donation to the Bay Area Women's Philharmonic. A mother of a 10-year-old boy, she contributes to groups with children's programs, such as the Oakland Public Library Association. "My husband and I tend to give to local groups on issues that are close to us, and to organizations we know something about."

Both personally and through her company, Peterson also supports the Women's Foundation, one of some 35 women's funds currently in operation. These funds, beginning with the Ms. Foundation for Women, established in 1972, are a response to traditional philanthropy's chronic underfinancing of women's issues. Today only 3.4 percent of private foundation money goes to women's and girls' projects (up from 0.6 percent in 1979). As Tracy Gary puts it: "Women should be supporting the women's funds; we can't depend on foundations, government, or corporations to do the work for us." Most of the funds operate on the local level, supporting the gamut of work in such feminist areas as child care, domestic violence, pay equity, and reproductive rights.

The national women's groups depend to a significant extent on membership dues and contributions from individuals. "Women should make their priorities clear," says Char Mollison, executive director of the Women's Equity Action League (WEAL), a nonprofit organization in Washington, D.C., that specializes in women's economic issues. "For the cost of a good pair of leather boots, you can join several national women's groups, support your local battered women's shelter, and save the whales at the same time."

Contributions to charities are tax-deductible, but only taxpayers who itemize get the deduction. By aggregating your gifts and donating once every two or three years, you may be able to qualify as an itemizer.

You can deduct no more than 50 percent of your adjusted gross income in charitable contributions in any one year. If your gift is appreciated property, such as securities or real estate, the amount you can deduct is 30 percent. Consult a tax accountant before making such gifts.

Tax-exempt organizations don't pay income taxes, but contributions to them aren't automatically tax-deductible. The charity's letter of determination and the IRS can tell you what is deductible.

If you receive goods or services—such as a prize or a meal—in return for your contribution, only the amount of your

74 Ms. December 1988

Illustration by Andrea Arroyo

Charities

3-D Illustrator: Andrea Arroyo
Art Director: Amy Bogart/Marlise Malkames
Publisher: Ms. Magazine
Client: Ms. Magazine
Category: Editorial Illustration

September 10, 1989 The New York Times Section 10A

Real Estate Report

Residential Property

First-Time Buyers Of Homes Face Hard Choices
Page 4

The Key to Appreciation, P. 10 • Confronting Sprawl, P. 16
Apartment Construction Chills, P. 26 • Table of Contents, P. 2

Copyright © 1989 The New York Times

Dream House

3-D Illustrator: Andrea Arroyo
Art Director: Richard Aloisio
Publisher: The New York Times Company
Client: The New York Times
Category: Editorial Illustration

Looking To The Stars

3-D Illustrator: Andrea Arroyo
Publisher: Theatreworks/USA
Client: Theatreworks/USA
Category: Advertising Illustration

Tempa Dot Ad

3-D Illustrator: Gordon Swenarton
Art Director: Frank Chesek
Photographer: Alan Levine
Agency: Falcone & Associates
Client: PyMaH Corporation
Category: Advertising Illustration

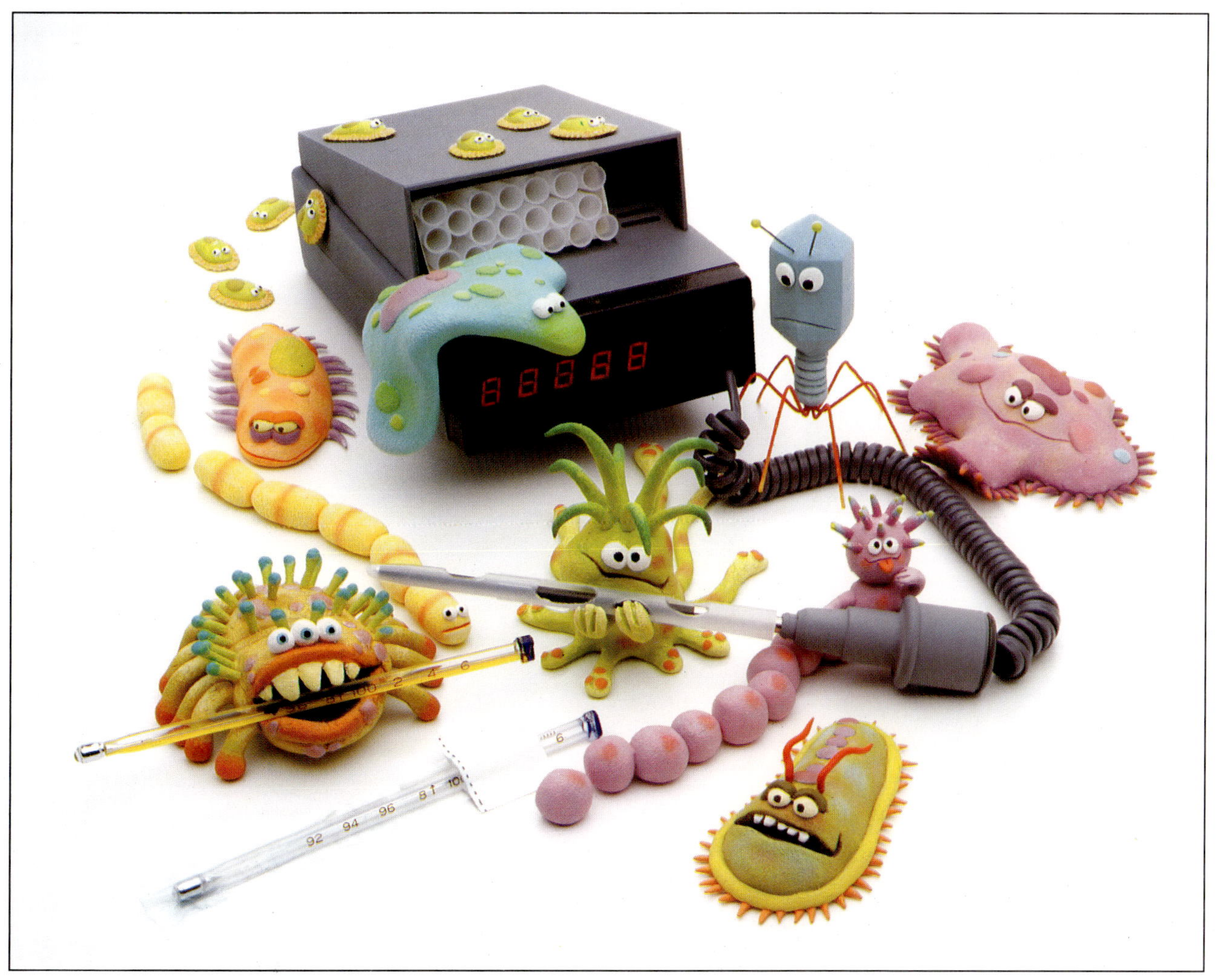

Art's Diner

3-D Illustrator: Tom Nachreiner
Art Director: Tom Nachreiner
Photographer: Ferdabar Studio
Agency: Art Factory
Client: Art Factory
Category: Calendar Full Page

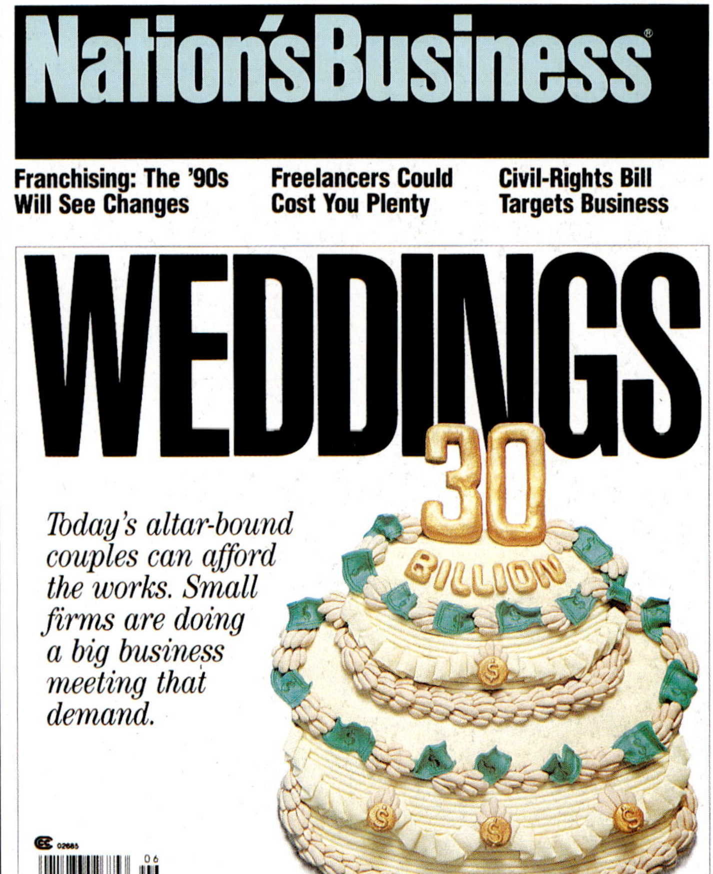

Weddings: The 30 Billion Dollar Business

3-D Illustrator: Doreen Gay-Kassel
Art Director: Hans Baum
Photographer: Franklin Gay
Publisher: Nations Business
Client: Nations Business
Category: Editorial Illustration

Lech Walensa

3-D Illustrator: Bob Selby
Art Director: Pete Coffey
Client: Providence Journal
Category: Editorial Illustration

Victoria Station

3-D Illustrator: Simi Berman
Photographer: Mats Nordstrom
Category: Editorial Illustration

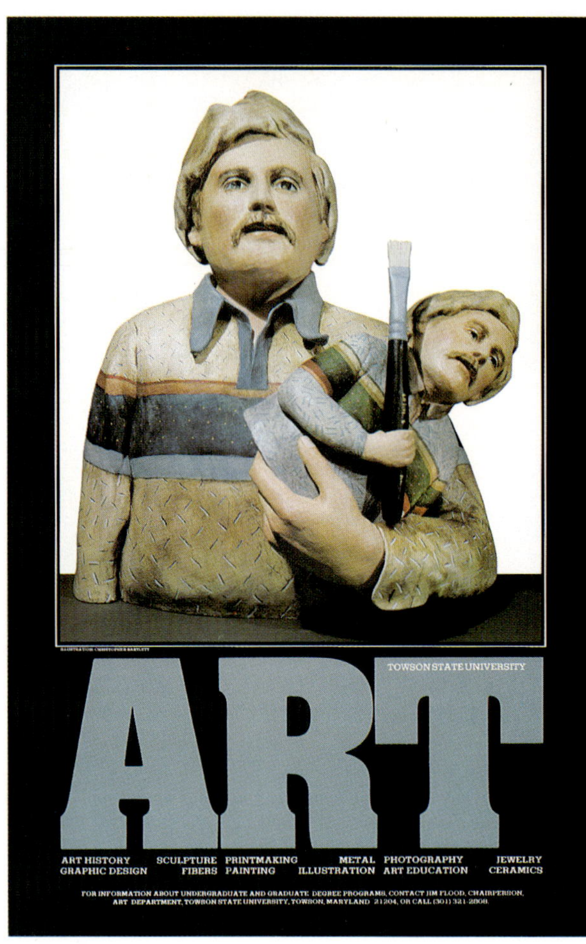

Self Portrait As Artist

3-D Illustrator: Christopher Bartlett
Art Director: Christopher Bartlett
Photographer: Christopher Bartlett
Agency: Bartlett & Associates
Publisher: Towson State University
Client: Towson State University
Category: Editorial Illustration

The Master

3-D Illustrator: Christopher Bartlett
Art Director: Christopher Bartlett
Photographer: Christopher Bartlett
Agency: Bartlett & Associates
Publisher: Towson State University
Client: Towson State University
Category: Editorial Illustration

Art Anyone?

3-D Illustrator: Christopher Bartlett
Art Director: Christopher Bartlett
Photographer: Christopher Bartlett
Agency: Bartlett & Associates
Publisher: Towson State University
Client: Towson State University
Category: Editorial Illustration

Pop Artist

3-D Illustrator: Christopher Bartlett
Art Director: Christopher Bartlett
Photographer: Christopher Bartlett
Agency: Bartlett & Associates
Publisher: Towson State University
Client: Towson State University
Category: Editorial Illustration

Small Businessman Extinct

3-D Illustrator: Jack Graham
Art Director: Jack Graham
Photographer: Bob Carey
Agency: Graham Illustration
Category: Editorial Illustration

Midnight Snack

3-D Illustrator: Jack Graham
Art Director: Jack Graham
Photographer: Bob Carey
Agency: Graham Illustration
Category: Advertising Illustration

Birds Of A Feather

3-D Illustrator: Mimi Foord
Art Director: Mimi Foord
Photographer: Keith Blohm Photography
Agency: Smaller Than Life Productions
Category: Unpublished

Parrot

3-D Illustrator: Jef Workman
Art Director: Jef Workman
Photographer: Mark Rice
Agency: Bird In The Hand
Category: Unpublished

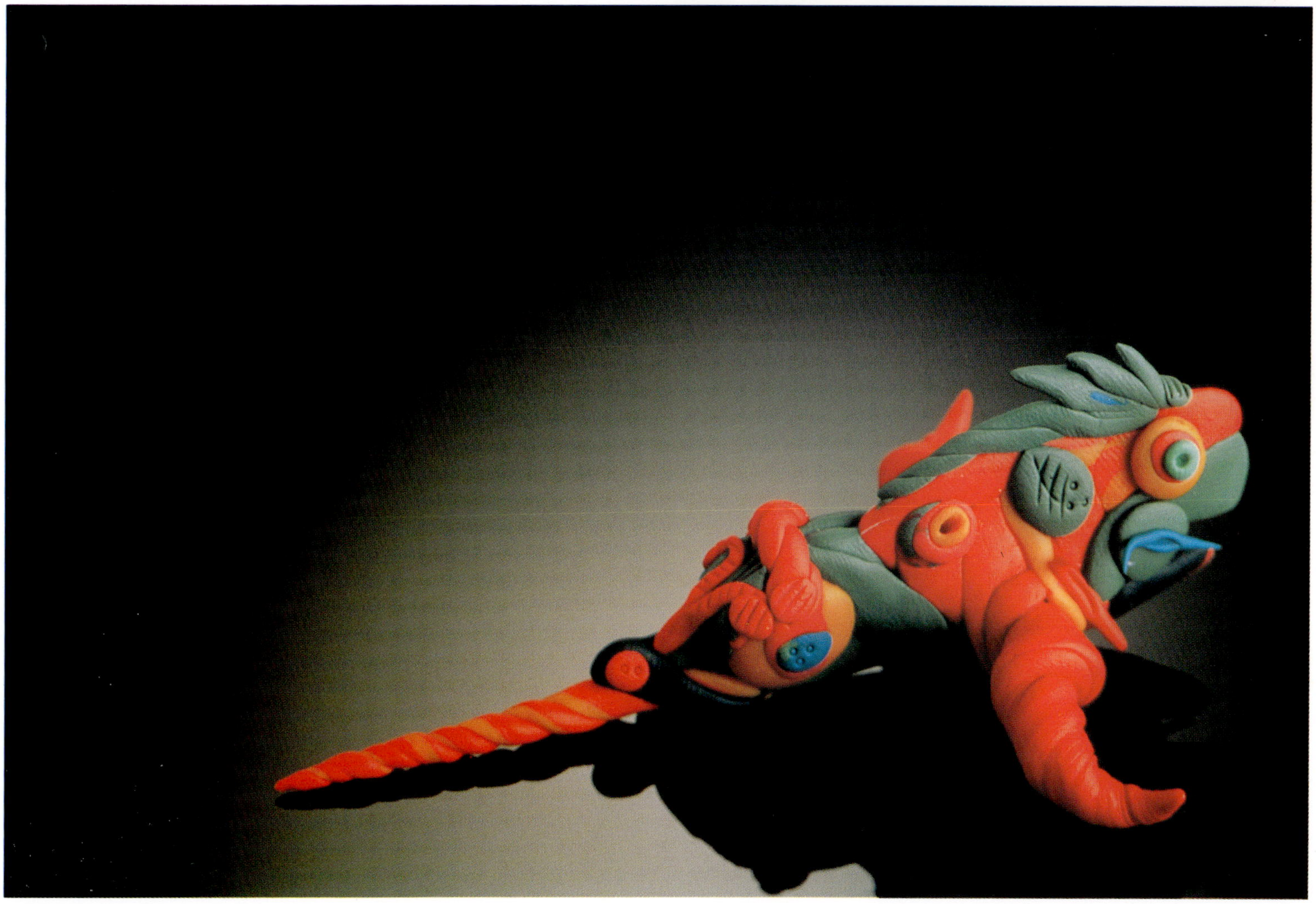

To Suit Your Appetite

3-D Illustrator: Mike Rosinski
Art Director: Mike Rosinski
Photographer: Jon Silla
Studio: John Lemmon Films
Publisher: John Lemmon Films
Client: John Lemmon Films
Category: Self Promotion Flyer

Street Poll

3-D Illustrator: Mary M. Bono
Photographer: Mary M. Bono
Client: Mary M. Bono
Category: Self Promotion Postcard

Reagan's Brainstorm

3-D Illustrator: Douglass Grimmett
Art Director: Douglass Grimmett
Photographer: Chuck Carlton
Category: Unpublished

Money To Lend

3-D Illustrator: Michael L. Goodman
Art Director: MaryAnn B. Collins
Photographer: Michael Pocklington
Publisher: James L. Dillon
MGB Communications, Inc.
Client: VA Business Magazine
Category: Consumer Magazine Full Page

Yogi Berra

3-D Illustrator: Mark L. Hazlerig
Art Director: Murry Tinkleman
Photographer: Mark L. Hazlerig
Agency: F/X Illustration
Publisher: Topps
Client: Topps Baseball Cards
Category: Miscellaneous

Dinosaur Mascot

3-D Illustrator: Kathy Jeffers
Art Director: Cindy Stone
Photographer: Chris Vincent
Agency: Southland Corporation/7-Eleven Stores
Client: Southland Corporation/7-Eleven Stores
Category: Miscellaneous

Bonkers

3-D Illustrator: Richard McNeel
Art Director: Nancy Finkenaur
Photographer: William G. Wagner
Publisher: The Milton Bradley Company
Client: The Milton Bradley Company
Category: Board Game

Bucket of Clay

3-D Illustrator: Mike Rosinski
Art Director: Mike Rosinski
Photographer: John Lemmon
Studio: John Lemmon Films
Client: John Lemmon Films
Publisher: John Lemmon Films
Category: Self Promotion Flyer

Casual T. Cat

Director: Mark Gustafson
Producer: Marilyn Zornado
Client: American Academy of Pediatrics
Category: Public Service

Dinosaur Grrrahams Pop-Up

Director: Mark Gustafson
Producer: Marilyn Zornado
Agency: Ketchum Advertising
Client: Mother's Cookies
Category: TV Commercial

Plastic is a relatively new illustrative medium. Technological advances have expanded the art director's options and increased the opportunities to bring creative concepts to fruition. The availability of acrylics, urethane, polymers and cast resins have augmented the capabilities of 3-D Illustrators to produce provocative high-tech imagery. The fusion of technical skills, with creative art direction, has resulted in the development of a singular illustrative artistry.

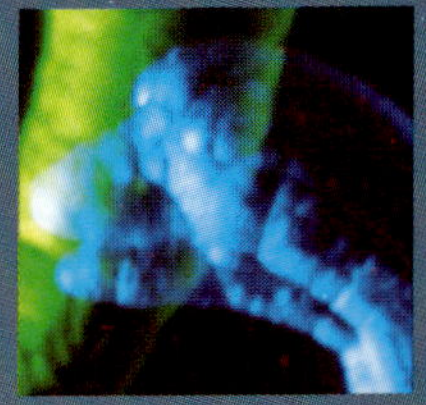

NANCY FOUTS
CROSSES † CRUCIFIXES
FOUTS & FOWLER
FOUTS & FOWLER GALLERY 30 TOTTENHAM STREET LONDON W1 9PN TELEPHONE 071-636 1064 FAX 071-388 6491

Archer

3-D Illustrator: Zoe Morsette/Jeffrey Muhs/Mark Yurkiw, Ltd.
Art Director: Mark Shap
Photographer: Matthew Rolston
Agency: Ogilvy & Mather, Inc.
Client: Cheesebrough-Ponds/Erno Laszlo-Seraph
Category: Advertising Consumer Magazine Full Page

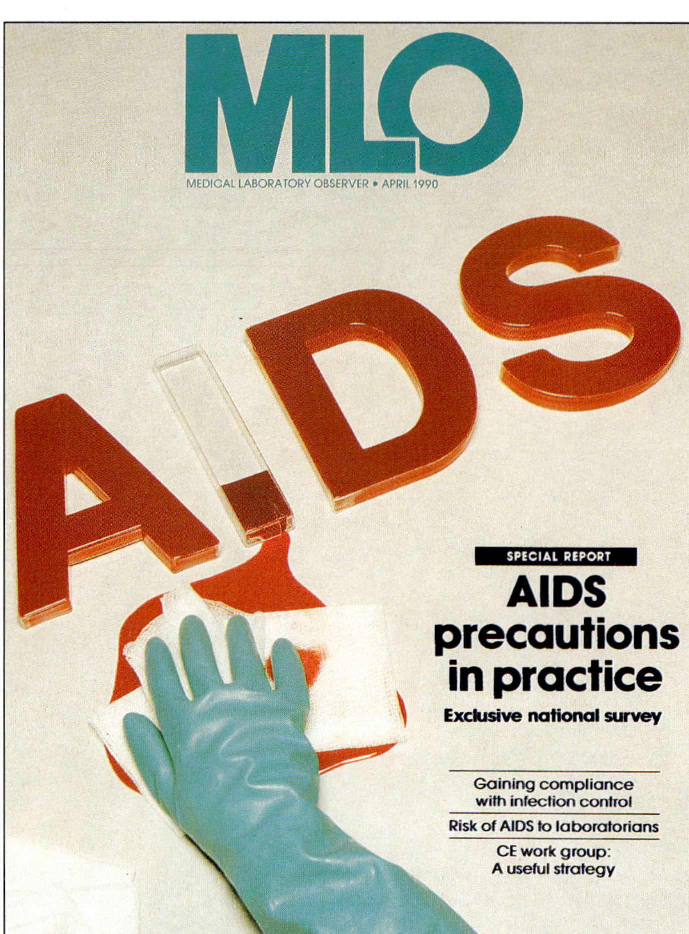

Aids Precautions In Practice

3-D Illustrator: Wellington Enterprises
Art Director: Kathleen Cuddihy
Photographer: Stephen E. Munz
Publisher: Medical Economics Company
Client: MLO
Category: Business Magazine Cover

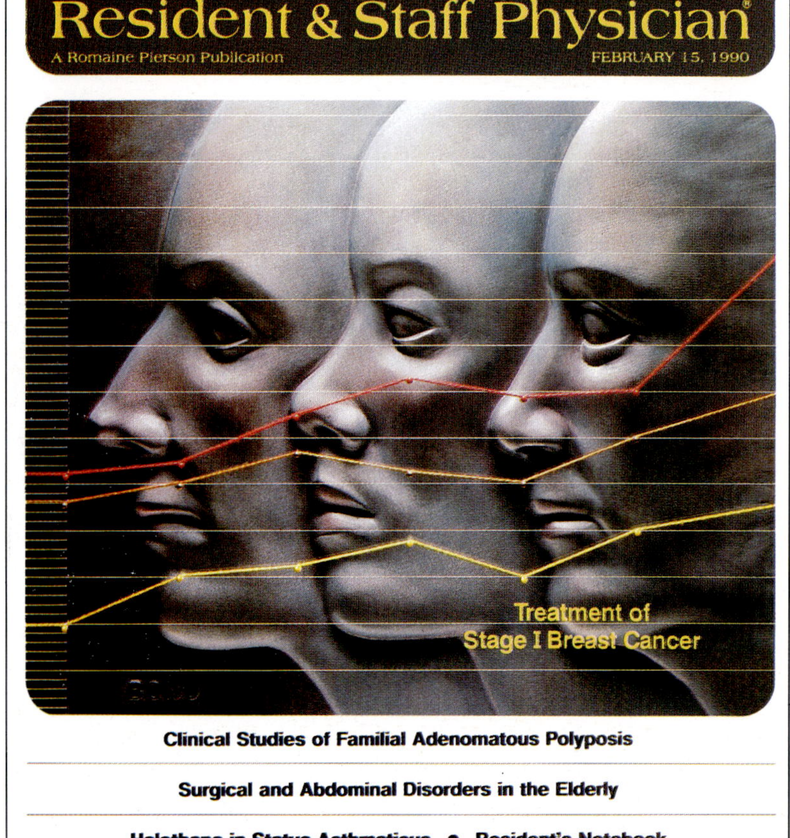

Treatment Of Stage I Breast Cancer

3-D Illustrator: Mary M. Bono
Art Director: Isabel Tavio
Photographer: Mary M. Bono
Publisher: Romaine Pierson Publishers, Inc.
Client: Resident & Staff Physician
Category: Business Magazine Cover

Computer Disc

3-D Illustrator: Mark L. Hazlerig
Art Director: Jason Noland/The Noland Group
Photographer: Ross Hickson
Agency: Hickson & Associates
Publisher: Macola Software
Client: Macola Software
Category: Advertising Business Direct Mail Brochure

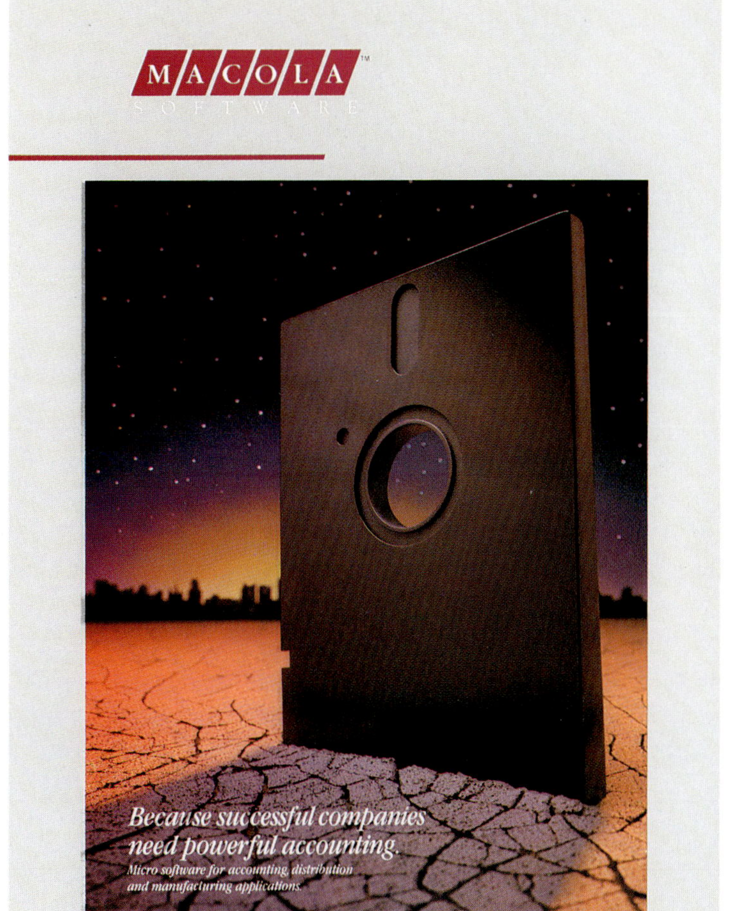

Forum Magazine

3-D Illustrator: Bob Emmott
Art Director: Jack Byrne/Dermot MacCormack
Photographer: Emmott Photography, Inc.
Agency: Design Resource, Inc.
Publisher: Intracorp
Client: Intracorp
Category: Business Magazine Cover

Bubble Gum Pack

3-D Illustrator: William Jackson/Mark Yurkiw, Ltd.
Art Director: Bruce Nilson
Photographer: Terry Niefield
Agency: FCB/Leber Katz Partners
Client: Planters Lifesavers Company/Care Free
Category: Advertising Consumer Magazine Full Page

Respiratory Distress Syndrome

3-D Illustrator: Nick Aristovulos
Art Director: Dick Russinko
Photographer: John Olivo/Al Parraga
Agency: Sudler & Hennessey
Publisher: Pioneer Moss, Engraver
Client: Burroughs Wellcome Company
Category: Advertising Business Magazine Full Page

Plastic City

3-D Illustrator: Bob Saint John
Art Director: Bob Saint John
Photographer: Bob Saint John
Client: LA Contemporary Art Fair
Category: Unpublished

1 + 1 = > 2

3-D Illustrator: The Object Works
Art Director: Craig Otto
Photographer: Bill Dutkovic
Agency: Dumun-Nelson & Company
Client: Urban Redevelopment Authority
Category: Advertising Direct Mail Poster

Emphysema, Chronic Bronchitis & Asthma

3-D Illustrator: Kathleen Ziegler
Art Director: Jeff Lipman
Photographer: Kathleen Ziegler
Agency: Thomas Ferguson Associates, Inc.
Client: Rorer Pharmaceuticals
Category: Advertising Business Direct Mail Brochure

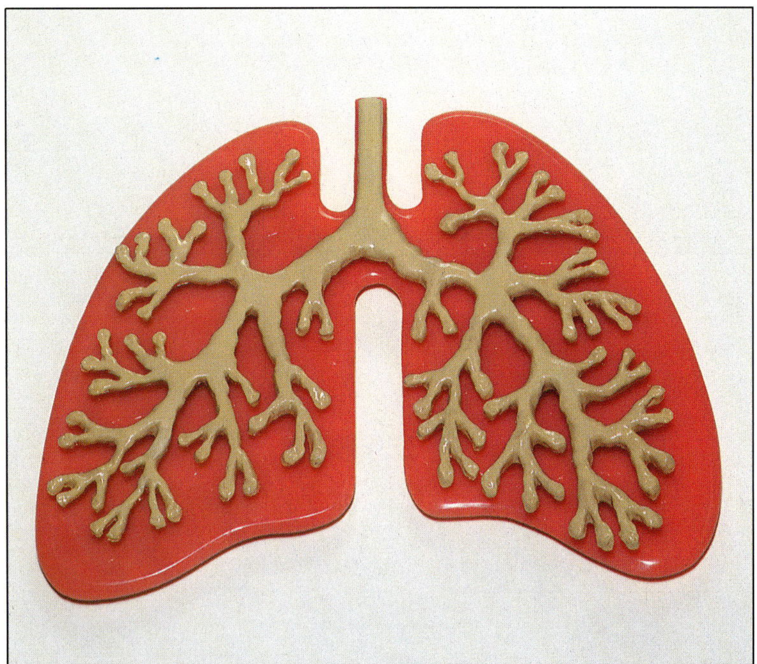

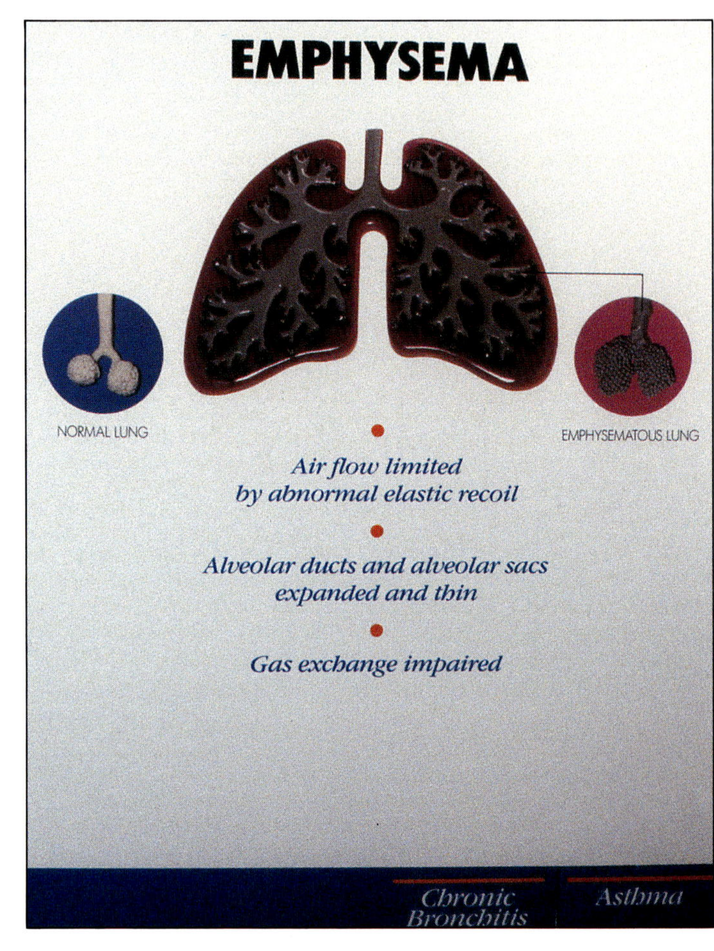

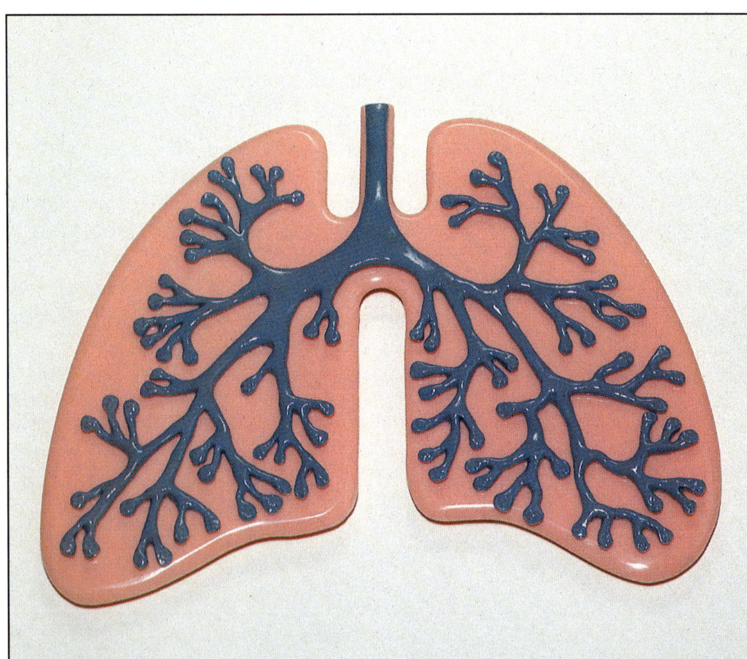

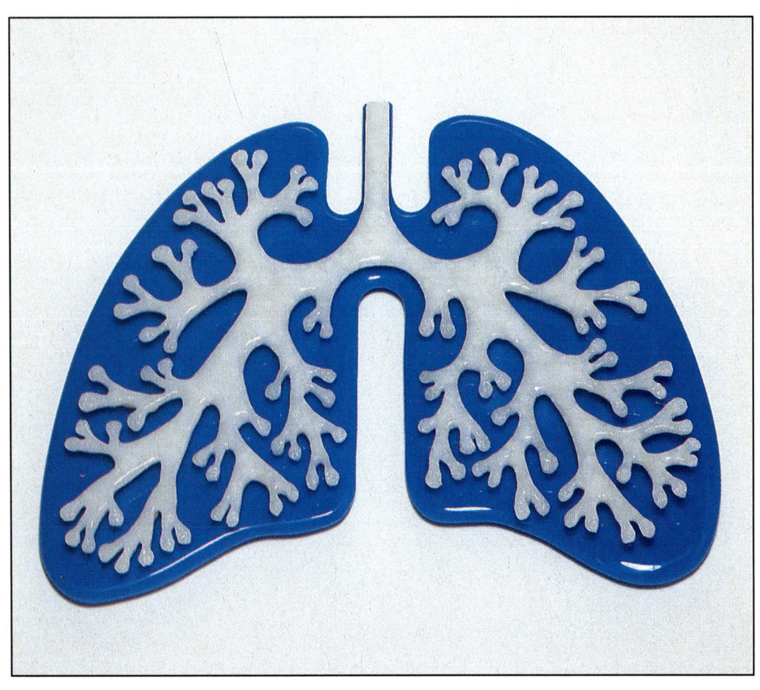

Cardiovascular System

3-D Illustrator: Bill Finewood
Art Director: Edmund Puches
Photographer: Bill Finewood
Agency: Puches Design
Client: Pfizer
Category: Miscellaneous

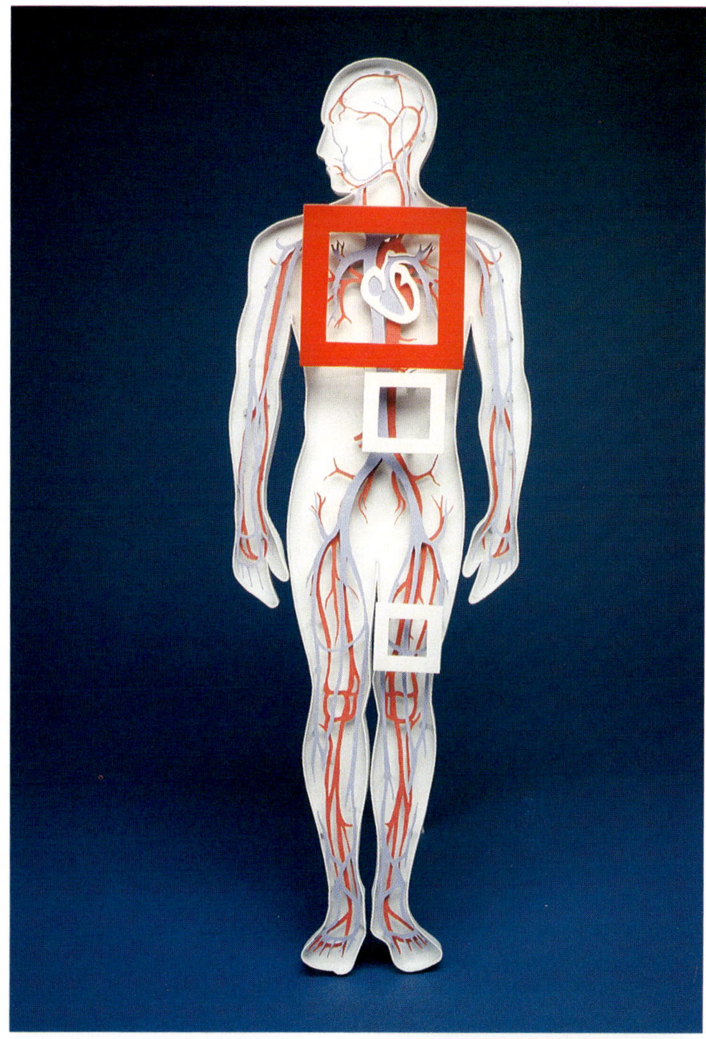

Urinary Tract

3-D Illustrator: Bill Finewood
Art Director: Edmund Puches
Photographer: Bill Finewood
Agency: Puches Design
Client: Pfizer
Category: Miscellaneous

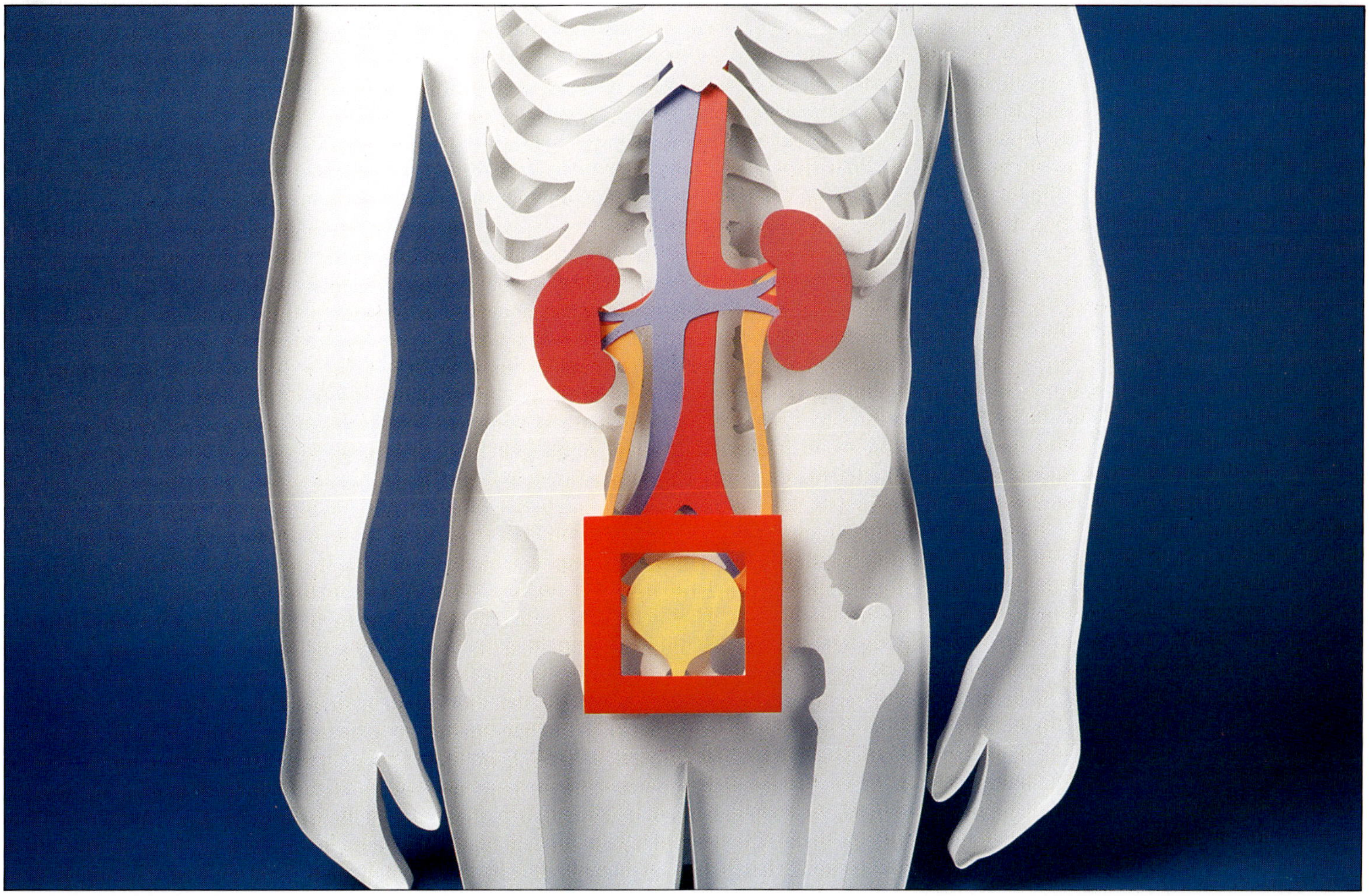

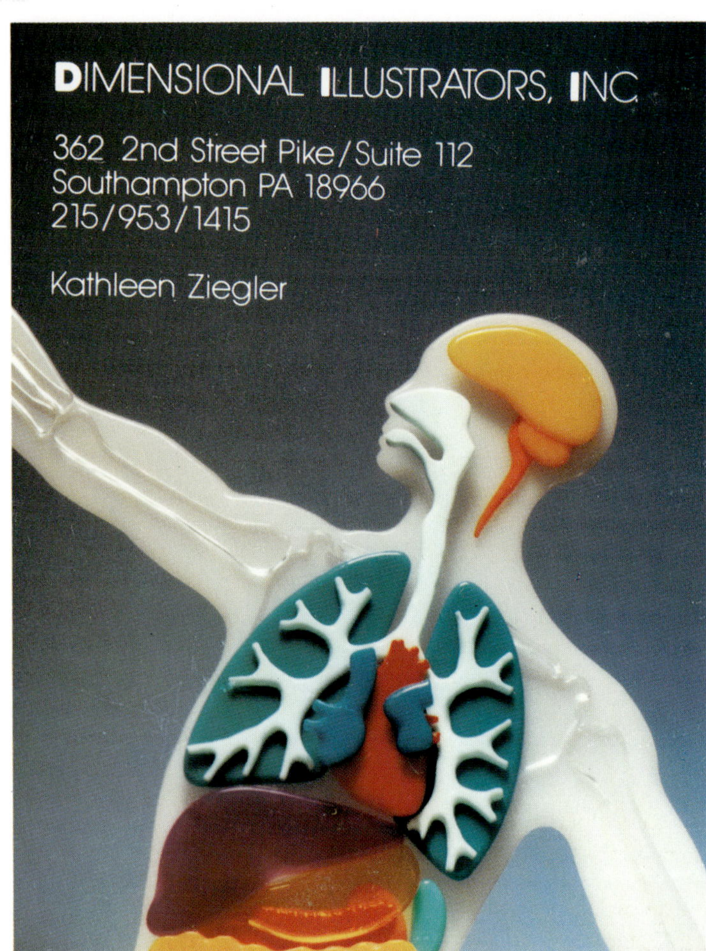

Body

3-D Illustrator: Kathleen Ziegler
Photographer: Kathleen Ziegler
Studio: Dimensional Illustrators, Inc.
Client: Dimensional Illustrators, Inc.
Category: Business Card

Reunification Of Germany

3-D Illustrator: Kathleen Ziegler
Art Director: Kathleen Ziegler
Photographer: Kathleen Ziegler
Studio: Dimensional Illustrators, Inc.
Category: Unpublished

Origin Of Species

3-D Illustrator: Kathleen Ziegler
Art Director: Kathleen Ziegler
Photographer: Kathleen Ziegler
Studio: Dimensional Illustrators, Inc.
Client: Academy of Natural Sciences
Category: Editorial Illustration

Glowing Brain

3-D Illustrator: Kathleen Ziegler
Art Director: Nick Greco
Photographer: Kathleen Ziegler
Studio: Dimensional Illustrators, Inc.
Category: Unpublished

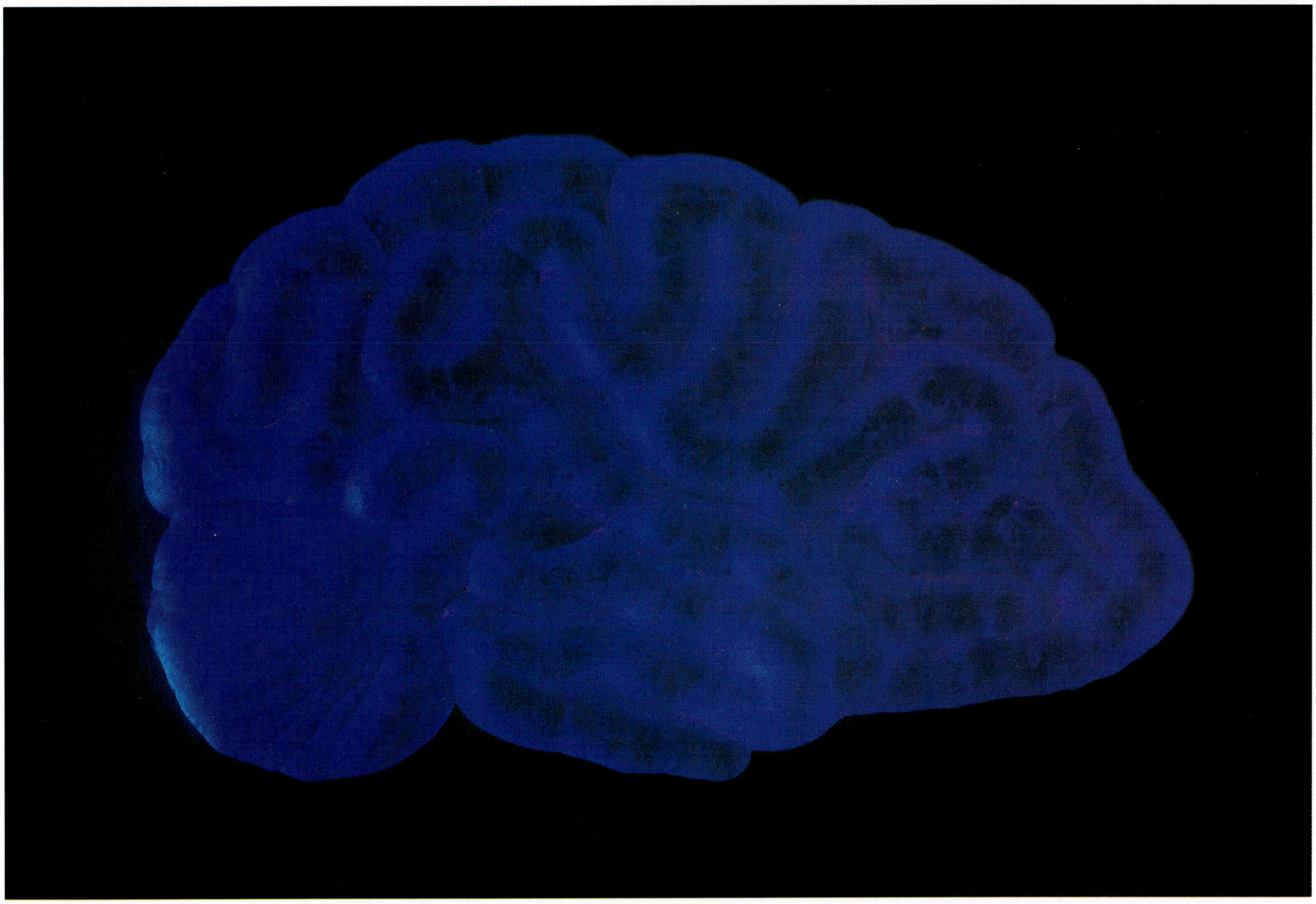

The singular medium classification validates the ingenuity and versatility of a particular application of 3-Dimensional Illustration. Art directors and modelmakers are using unconventional mediums that reflect a spontaneity and uniqueness that is unencumbered by traditional flat illustration. Models are created in a variety of mediums including metal, copper, sand, food, stone, latex and wax. Products such as soap, chocolate, cigarettes, and dog bones have been used as illustrative mediums to entice the viewer's interest. This singular class of illustration gives the 3-D image-maker the creative license to explore an infinite variety of 3-D mediums.

Smirnoff Egyptian Ad

3-D Illustrator: Malcolm Fowler
Art Director: Ruth Owen

The Christmas Story Marley

3-D Illustrator: Todd Vanderpluym
Art Director: Todd Vanderpluym
Photographer: Chad Slattery
Agency: Santa Anita Park
Client: Santa Anita Park
Category: Miscellaneous
Medium: Sand Sculpture

The Pillars Of The Earth

3-D Illustrator: Achim Kiel
Art Director: Arno Haering
Photographer: Uwe Brandes
Agency: Pencil Corporate Art
Publisher: Gustav Luebbe Verlag GmbH
Client: Gustav Luebbe Verlag GmbH
Category: Book Cover

Lighted House

3-D Illustrator: Olive Alpert
Art Director: Herb Bleiweiss
Photographer: Olive Alpert

JANUARY 1, 1990 $2.50
MAN OF THE DECADE
TIME
Mikhail Gorbachev

Gorbachev Man Of The Decade

3-D Illustrator: Hans Limbach
Art Director: Rudolph C. Hoglund
Photographer: Roberto Brosan
Publisher: Time Warner, Inc.
Category: Consumer Magazine Cover

Monster Mask

3-D Illustrator: Scott Molampy
Art Director: Al Nagy
Photographer: Nick Koudis
Publisher: Childrens Television Workshop
Client: 321 Contact Magazine
Category: Consumer Magazine Spread
Medium: Foam Sculpture

Rambush

3-D Illustrator: Bob Selby
Art Director: Pete Coffey
Photographer: Dick Benjamin
Publisher: Providence Journal
Client: Providence Journal
Category: Editorial Illustration
Medium: Paper Mache

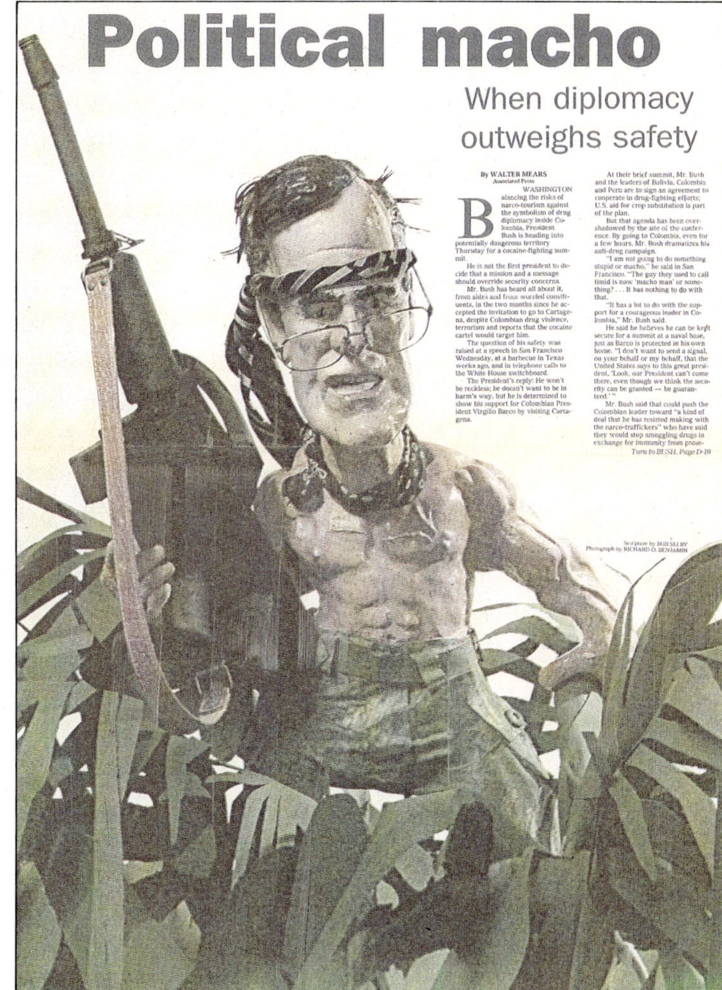

Political macho

When diplomacy outweighs safety

By WALTER MEARS
Associated Press

WASHINGTON

Balancing the risks of narco-tourism against the symbolism of drug diplomacy inside Colombia, President Bush is heading into potentially dangerous territory Thursday for a cocaine-fighting summit.

He is not the first president to decide that a mission and a message should override security concerns.

Mr. Bush has heard all about it, from aides and from worried constituents, in the two months since he accepted the invitation to go to Cartagena, despite Colombian drug violence, terrorism and reports that the cocaine cartel would target him.

The question of his safety was raised at a speech in San Francisco Wednesday, at a barbecue in Texas weeks ago, and in telephone calls to the White House switchboard.

The President's reply: He won't be reckless; he doesn't want to be in harm's way, but he is determined to show his support for Colombian President Virgilio Barco by visiting Cartagena.

At their brief summit, Mr. Bush and the leaders of Bolivia, Colombia and Peru are to sign an agreement to cooperate in drug-fighting efforts; U.S. aid for crop substitution is part of the plan.

But that agenda has been overshadowed by the site of the conference. By going to Colombia, even for a few hours, Mr. Bush dramatizes his anti-drug campaign.

"I am not going to do something stupid or macho," he said in San Francisco. "The guy they used to call timid is now 'macho man' or something? . . . It has nothing to do with that.

"It has a lot to do with the support for a courageous leader in Colombia," Mr. Bush said.

He said he believes he can be kept secure for a summit at a naval base, just as Barco is protected in his own home. "I don't want to send a signal, on your behalf or my behalf, that the United States says to this great president, 'Look, our President can't come there, even though we think the security can be granted — be guaranteed.'"

Mr. Bush said that could push the Colombian leader toward "a kind of deal that he has resisted making with the narco-traffickers" who have said they would stop smuggling drugs in exchange for immunity from prose-

Turn to BUSH, Page D-10

Sculpture by BOB SELBY
Photograph by RICHARD O. BENJAMIN

Steel Recycling

3-D Illustrator: The Object Works
Art Director: Dave Hughes
Photographer: Walt Seng
Agency: Ketchum Advertising, Pittsburgh
Client: American Iron & Steel Institute
Category: Advertising Business Magazine Spread
Medium: Metal Sculpture

Why The Steel Can Is More Attractive For Recycling.

It's one of the most basic ideas in physics. Magnetism. And it's why the new steel can is making a remarkable comeback in this age of growing concern over the environment, and growing interest in recycling.

You see, because steel is magnetic (in contrast to other recyclable materials), it can be easily extracted from municipal waste. A greater savings to both municipalities and recyclers. With greater reclamation and less expense than payback and deposit programs.

There's Strength In Steel's Growing Numbers.

You might not have guessed it, but steel is 100% recyclable and 100% degradable, creating no environmental hazards. Which is why more people are using and recycling steel cans.

In fact, 66% of all steel manufactured in 1988 was from recycled product. And 15% of all steel cans produced are eventually recycled.

And Perhaps Even Greater Strength In Our Design And Reliability.

The strength and durability of steel cans are legendary.

But for everyday applications and hazards, they're indispensable. Steel's protection is simply unequalled. And steel cans still offer you light weight, two-piece seamless can designs with less cost, reduced rejects and lower secondary spoilage.

The New Steel Can. It's The Cost Container. And The Environmental Protector.

To find out more about steel recycling, call the Steel Can Recycling Institute at 1-800-876-SCRI. In Canada, call the Canadian Tinplate Recycling Council at (416) 528-2386.

The Future Is Contained In Recyclable Steel
American Iron And Steel Institute
AISI, 1133 15th Street, NW
Washington, D.C. 20005-2701
(202) 452-7100, FAX: (202) 463-6573

Steel the recycled material

Handbook For AGD

3-D Illustrator: Achim Kiel
Art Director: Achim Kiel
Photographer: Uwe Brandes
Agency: Pencil Corporate Art
Publisher: Allianz Deutscher Designer AGD
Client: Allianz Deutscher Designer AGD
Category: Annual Report Cover
Medium: Wood/Metal

Pasta Ship

3-D Illustrator: Mark Yurkiw, Ltd.
Art Director: Chuck Finkle
Photographer: Lou Wallach
Agency: Ogilvy & Mather, Inc.
Client: American Express Publishing/Food & Wine
Category: Advertising Consumer Magazine Spread
Medium: Food Sculpture

High Strength

3-D Illustrator: The Object Works
Art Director: Ed Macko
Photographer: John Sanderson
Agency: Vandine Humphrey
Client: Jessop Steel
Category: Advertising Business Magazine Full Page
Medium: Wax Sculpture

Vegetable Watch

3-D Illustrator: Mark Yurkiw, Ltd.
Art Director: Chuck Finkle
Photographer: Lou Wallach
Agency: Ogilvy & Mather, Inc.
Client: American Express Publishing/Food & Wine
Category: Advertising Consumer Magazine Spread
Medium: Food Sculpture

Mom And Son Soap Ad

3-D Illustrator: Malcolm Fowler
Art Director: Henry Rossitier
Photographer: Charles Stebbings
Agency: Young & Rubicam London
Client: Palmolive
Category: Advertising Illustration
Medium: Wax Sculpture

Boneo Doggy

3-D Illustrator: Nancy Fouts
Art Director: Nancy Fouts
Photographer: Nancy Fouts
Agency: Shirt Sleeve Studio London
Category: Unpublished
Medium: Dog Bones

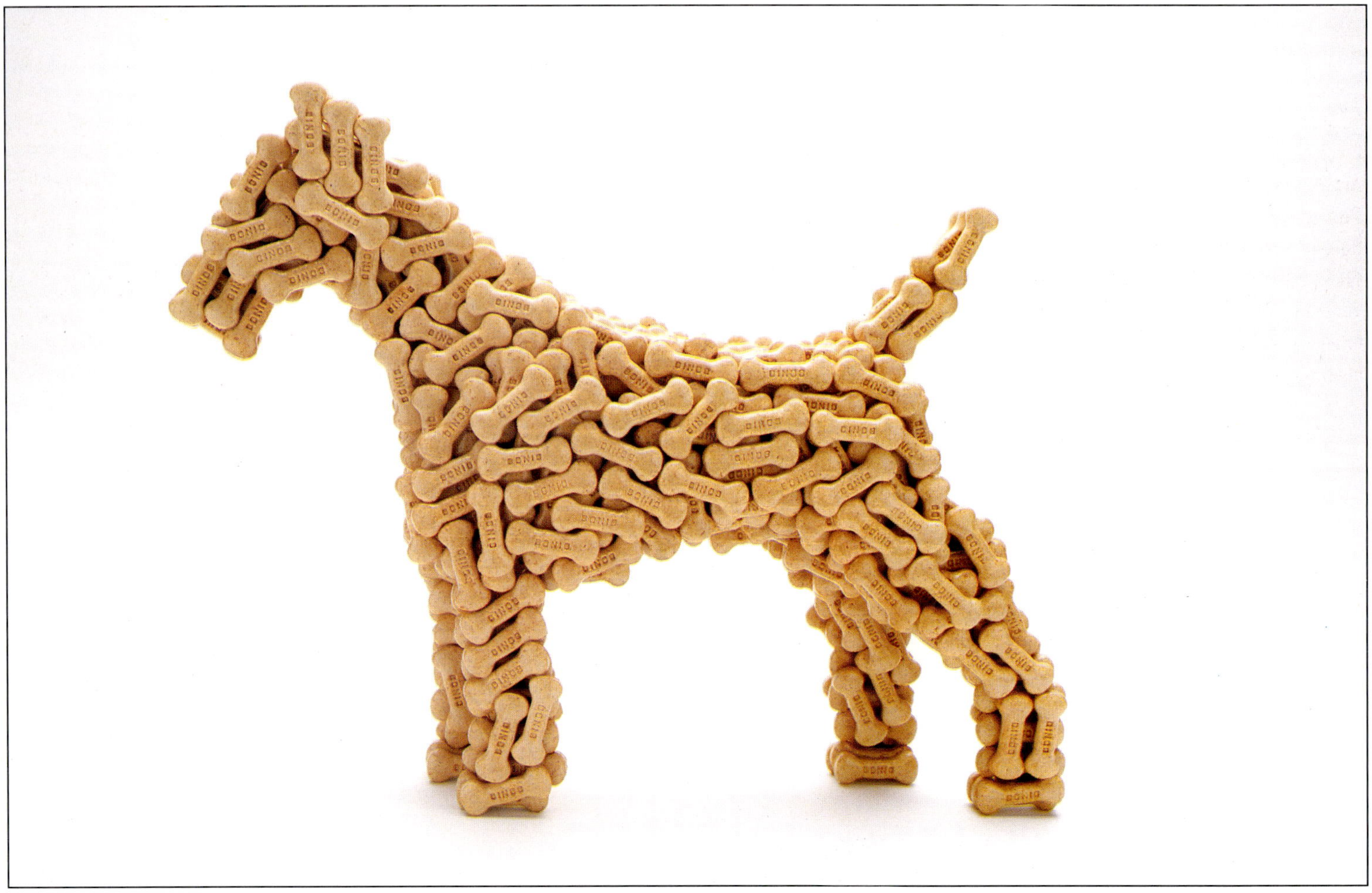

Jocko

3-D Illustrator: Bonnie Rasmussen
Art Director: Bonnie Rasmussen
Photographer: Sauer & Associates
Agency: A.Art/B.Rasmussen, Ltd.
Client: SUPPORT DOGS For The Handicapped, Inc.
St. Louis, MO
Category: Miscellaneous
Medium: Metal Sculpture

Big John

3-D Illustrator: Bill Miller
Photographer: Bill Miller
Category: Unpublished
Medium: Copper Sculpture

Foam Props

3-D Illustrator: Bob Field
Photographer: Bob Kramer Studio/Bill Leatherman Studio
Category: Self Promotion Campaign
Medium: Foam Sculpture

Slice Of Lemon Cake

3-D Illustrator: Rosemary Littman
Art Director: Rosemary Littman
Photographer: Rosemary Littman
Category: Unpublished
Medium: Cake & Icing

Coo-Coo Clock

3-D Illustrator: Olive Alpert
Art Director: Herb Bleiweiss
Photographer: Victor Scocozza
Publisher: Hearst
Client: Good Housekeeping
Category: Unpublished
Medium: Gingerbread

Lettuce, Tomatoes & Crudites Cake

3-D Illustrator: Rosemary Littman
Art Director: Rosemary Littman
Photographer: Rosemary Littman
Category: Unpublished
Medium: Cake & Icing

Grandfather Clock

3-D Illustrator: Olive Alpert
Art Director: Herb Bleiweiss
Photographer: Victor Scocozza
Publisher: Hearst
Client: Good Housekeeping
Category: Unpublished
Medium: Gingerbread

Balls Of Yarn Cake

3-D Illustrator: Rosemary Littman
Art Director: Rosemary Littman
Photographer: Rosemary Littman
Category: Unpublished
Medium: Cake & Icing

German Old Rafter Gingerbread House

3-D Illustrator: Olive Alpert
Art Director: Herb Bleiweiss
Photographer: Victor Scocozza
Publisher: Hearst
Client: Good Housekeeping
Category: Unpublished
Medium: Gingerbread

Merry Christmas Gingerbread House

3-D Illustrator: Olive Alpert
Art Director: Herb Bleiweiss
Photographer: Victor Scocozza
Publisher: Hearst
Client: Good Housekeeping
Category: Unpublished
Medium: Gingerbread

Christmas Bird House

3-D Illustrator: Olive Alpert
Art Director: Herb Bleiweiss
Photographer: Victor Scocozza
Publisher: Hearst
Client: Good Housekeeping
Category: Unpublished
Medium: Gingerbread

Brick Mansion

3-D Illustrator: Olive Alpert
Art Director: Herb Bleiweiss
Photographer: Victor Scocozza
Publisher: Hearst
Client: Good Housekeeping
Category: Unpublished
Medium: Gingerbread

Geodesic Pineapple House

3-D Illustrator: Olive Alpert
Art Director: Olive Alpert
Photographer: Olive Alpert
Client: Design Industry Foundation For Aids
Category: Miscellaneous
Medium: Gingerbread

Frankenstein-Mary Shelley 1818

3-D Illustrator: Mark L. Hazlerig
Art Director: Mark L. Hazlerig
Photographer: Mark L. Hazlerig
Agency: F/X Illustration
Category: Unpublished
Medium: Latex/Foam

Tiny Tim And Family

3-D Illustrator: Todd Vanderpluym
Art Director: Todd Vanderpluym
Photographer: Chad Slattery
Agency: Santa Anita Park
Client: Santa Anita Park
Category: Miscellaneous
Medium: Sand Sculpture

The Christmas Story Scrooge

3-D Illustrator: Todd Vanderpluym
Art Director: Todd Vanderpluym
Photographer: Chad Slattery
Agency: Santa Anita Park
Client: Santa Anita Park
Category: Miscellaneous
Medium: Sand Sculpture

Santa Swing On A Snowflake

3-D Illustrator: Olive Alpert
Art Director: Herb Bleiweiss
Photographer: Olive Alpert
Publisher: Hearst
Client: Good Housekeeping
Category: Unpublished
Medium: Gingerbread

Santa Pushing Sled Uphill

3-D Illustrator: Olive Alpert
Art Director: Olive Alpert
Photographer: Olive Alpert
Client: Olive Alpert
Category: Greeting Card
Medium: Gingerbread

Mad Scientist

3-D Illustrator: Carolyn Daley
Art Director: Mark L. Hazlerig
Photographer: Robert Groh
Agency: Columbus College of Art and Design
Category: Unpublished
Medium: Latex/Foam
Student: Columbus College of Art and Design

Ethal

3-D Illustrator: Susan Klumpp
Art Director: Mark Hazlerig
Photographer: Susan Klumpp
Category: Unpublished
Medium: Latex/Foam
Student: Columbus College of Art and Design

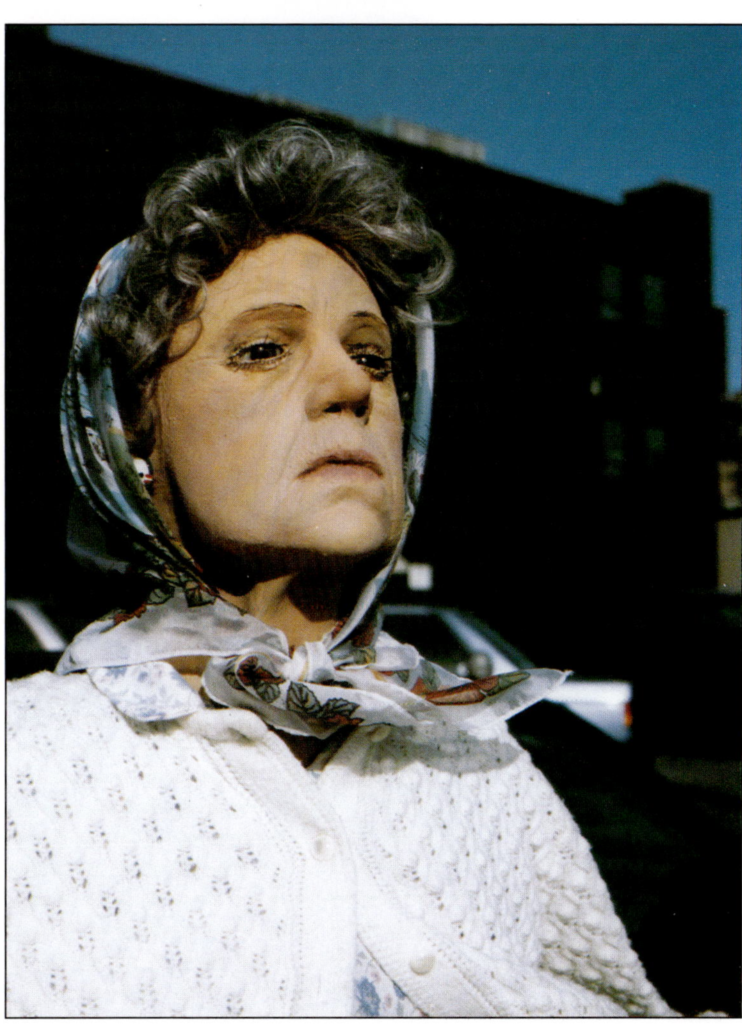

The unique imagery of paper collage makes it an innovative form of 3-Dimensional Illustration. Cut paper, torn paper and photo collage techniques are used to create subtle 3-D images. The nuances of tone, texture and shape are captured by this most delicate form of 3-Dimensional Illustration. Though considered a minimal style of 3-D Illustration, the contributions of paper collage to the third dimension are notable. Today, paper collage is making major strides in the visual communications industry.

S I L V E R

Cultural Events

3-D Illustrator: Achim Kiel
Art Director: Juergen Peters
Photographer: Uwe Brandes
Agency: Pencil Corporate Art
Publisher: Magazinpresse
Client: Westermann's

Performing Arts In New York

3-D Illustrator: Marti Shohet
Photographer: Richard Freed
Publisher: Creative Illustration Annual

Dating: How Do You Do That?

3-D Illustrator: Cecily Lang
Art Director: Rob Molthoff
Publisher: Swets & Zeitlinger BV
Client: Psychologie
Category: Consumer Magazine Full Page

A Changing Climate

3-D Illustrator: Susan Nichols
Art Director: Ann Wolf
Publisher: Palm Beach Life Magazine
Client: Palm Beach Life Magazine
Category: Business Magazine Full Page

Token Ring

3-D Illustrator: Carol H. Norby
Art Director: Kate Johnson
Publisher: McGraw Hill
Client: NetWare Technical Journal
Category: Business Magazine Full Page

Merpersons

3-D Illustrator: Joan Hall
Art Director: Marshall Harmon
Agency: Harmon, Kemp, Inc.
Client: International Paper Company
Category: Advertising Business Direct Mail Poster

Publishing In Paradise

3-D Illustrator: Susan Nichols
Art Director: Ann Wolf
Publisher: Palm Beach Life Magazine
Client: Palm Beach Life Magazine
Category: Business Magazine Cover

A View Of Monte Carlo

3-D Illustrator: Marti Shohet
Art Director: Steven Visconti
Photographer: Richard Freed
Agency: Muir, Cornelius, Moore
Client: Payne Weber
Category: Advertising Business Direct Mail Postcard

The Caretakers
SIERRA CLUB
Name
Alt. above Sea L
Basket Dome
Cathedral Rocks
Cathedral Spires
Clouds Rest
REPORT
ACTING SUPERINT
YOSEMITE NATIO
CALIFORN
YOSEMITE VALLEY
NATIONAL PARK SERVICE
RULES AND REGULATIONS
Park.

The Residents
INDIANS of the Yosemite

The Naturalists and Scientists
Amphibians and Reptiles..............29 species
Birds..............223 species
Fish (six natural species)..............11 species
Mammals..............77 species
BIG TREES
A YOSEMITE FLORA
HANDBOOK OF YOSEMITE NATIONAL PARK

Yosemite 100

3-D Illustrator: Laura Tarrish
Art Director: Bob Kosturak/Laura Tarrish
Agency: Ancona & Associates
Publisher: California Academy of Sciences
Client: California Academy of Sciences
Category: Business Magazine Campaign

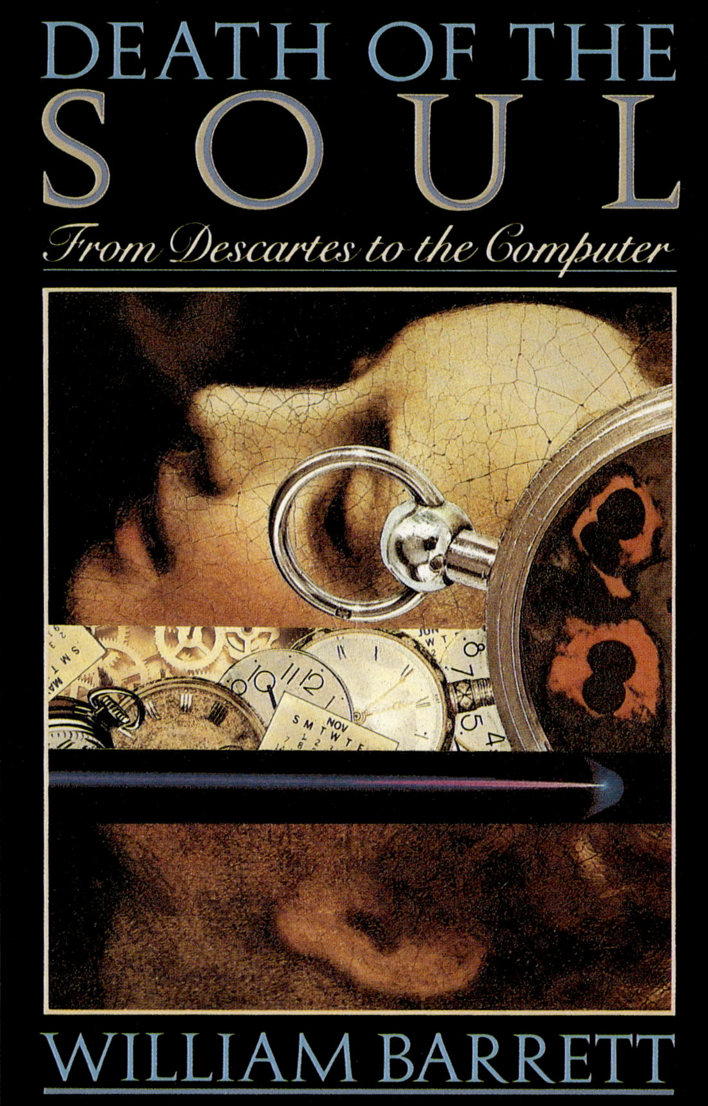

Death Of The Soul

3-D Illustrator: Joan Hall
Art Director: Doug Bergstreser
Publisher: Doubleday Anchor
Category: Book Cover

Strangers In Paradox

3-D Illustrator: Carol H. Norby
Art Director: Julie Easton
Publisher: Signature Books
Client: Signature Books
Category: Book Cover

Writing Is Critical Action

3-D Illustrator: Laura Tarrish
Art Director: Jackie Kolb/Lucy Lesiak
Agency: Lucy Lesiak Design
Publisher: Scott Foresman & Company
Client: Scott Foresman & Company
Category: Book Cover

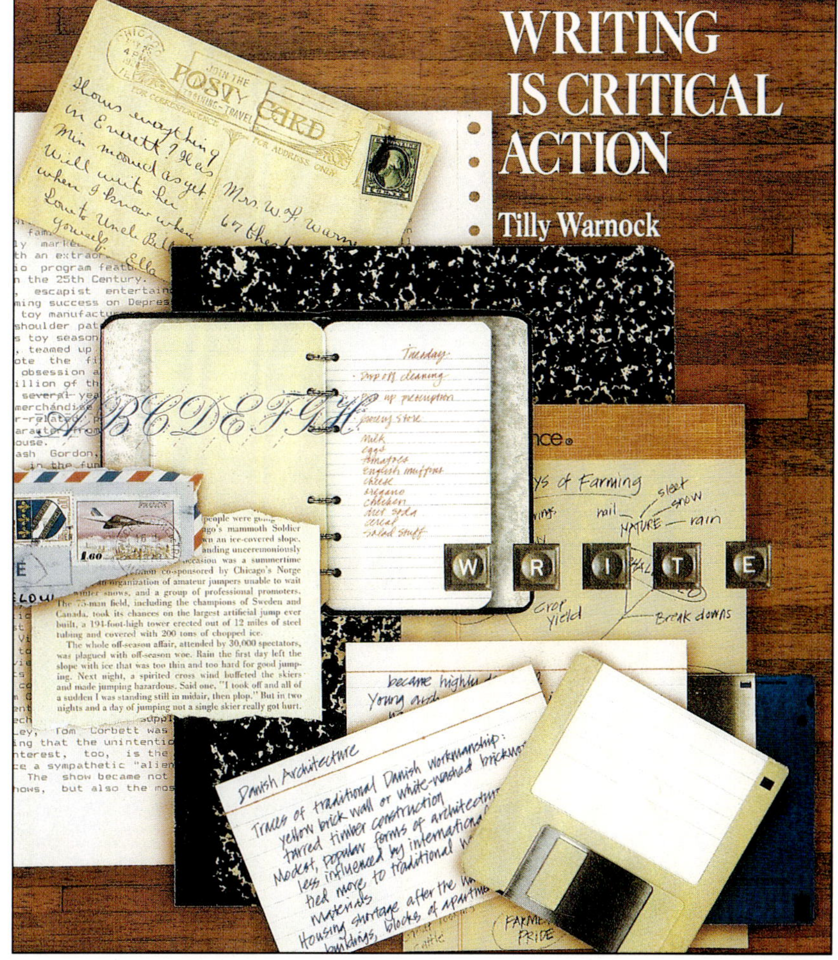

Making Sense Of The Region's Growth

3-D Illustrator: Laura Tarrish
Art Director: Sharon Till/Laura Tarrish
Agency: Sharon Till Design
Client: The Bay Area Council
Category: Annual Report Cover

Novations

3-D Illustrator: Carol H. Norby
Art Director: Randall Smith
Agency: Randall Smith Associates
Client: Novations
Category: Advertising Business Direct Mail Brochure

The Access Standard

3-D Illustrator: Carol H. Norby
Art Director: Larry Clarkson
Agency: Clarkson-Twede
Client: Century Software
Category: Advertising Illustration

If You've Got It, Flaunt It

3-D Illustrator: Marie Corfield
Art Director: Marie Corfield
Photographer: William Wagner
Category: Unpublished

Animals Of The Jungle

3-D Illustrator: Jennine Vainisi
Client: Jennine Vainisi
Category: Unpublished

Post-Partum Depression

3-D Illustrator: Marti Shohet
Art Director: Richard Loretoni
Photographer: Richard Freed
Publisher: Gruner & Jahr
Client: Parents Magazine
Category: Editorial Illustration

Still Life With Violin

3-D Illustrator: Marti Shohet
Photographer: Richard Freed
Category: Self Promotion Flyer

Several Generations

3-D Illustrator: Cathy Saksa
Art Director: Cathy Saksa
Publisher: AT&T
Category: Editorial Illustration

Borderline

3-D Illustrator: Cathy Saksa
Art Director: Neil Stuart
Publisher: Viking Publishers
Category: Unpublished

20th Anniversary Of Moon Landing

3-D Illustrator: Cathy Saksa
Art Director: Marion Smith
Publisher: Newsweek Sunday Magazine
Category: Editorial Illustration

Dream Game

3-D Illustrator: Cathy Saksa
Art Director: Gene Mydlowski
Publisher: Harper & Row, Inc.
Category: Self Promotion Flyer

Carnival

3-D Illustrator: Cecily Lang
Publisher: American Showcase
Category: Unpublished

Fish

3-D Illustrator: Cecily Lang
Publisher: American Showcase
Category: Unpublished

Fashion Statement

3-D Illustrator: Bob Saint John
Art Director: Bob Saint John
Photographer: Bob Saint John
Publisher: Turnbull & Company
Client: Worksource
Category: Self Promotion Flyer

The Merry Tree

3-D Illustrator: Susan Baum
Publisher: Harper & Row
Category: Complete Book

hope

peace

Perfume Ad

3-D Illustrator: Marie Corfield
Art Director: Marie Corfield
Photographer: William Wagner
Category: Unpublished

Pencil Drawing

3-D Illustrator: Marie Corfield
Art Director: Marie Corfield
Photographer: William Wagner
Category: Unpublished

Cow Carton

3-D Illustrator: Jill Kagan Batelman
Art Director: Jill Kagan Batelman
Photographer: Jill Kagan Batelman
Category: Unpublished

World's Largest Chicken

3-D Illustrator: Jill Kagan Batelman
Art Director: Jill Kagan Batelman
Photographer: Jill Kagan Batelman
Category: Unpublished

Wood as a sculptural medium dates back to Egyptian times. Today, wood sculpture is recognized as a viable 3-Dimensional Illustration medium. The natural texture and tonal variations are ideally suited for the creation of aesthetically appealing 3-Dimensional models and props. Low-relief carvings and free-standing sculpture, demonstrate the versatility and beauty of wood. Talented creatives, cognizant of the impact of 3-Dimensional Illustration, are using wood sculpture as a creative medium for illustration.

Black Palm Cockatoo

3-D Illustrator: Nancy Blauers
Art Director: Nancy Blauers
Photographer: Maurice Sherman
Category: Self Promotion Postcard

Gangs

3-D Illustrator: Joe Fleming
Art Director: Gary Stuber
Photographer: See Spot Run
Agency: Project X
Publisher: Applied Arts Quarterly
Client: Joe Fleming
Category: Advertising Illustration

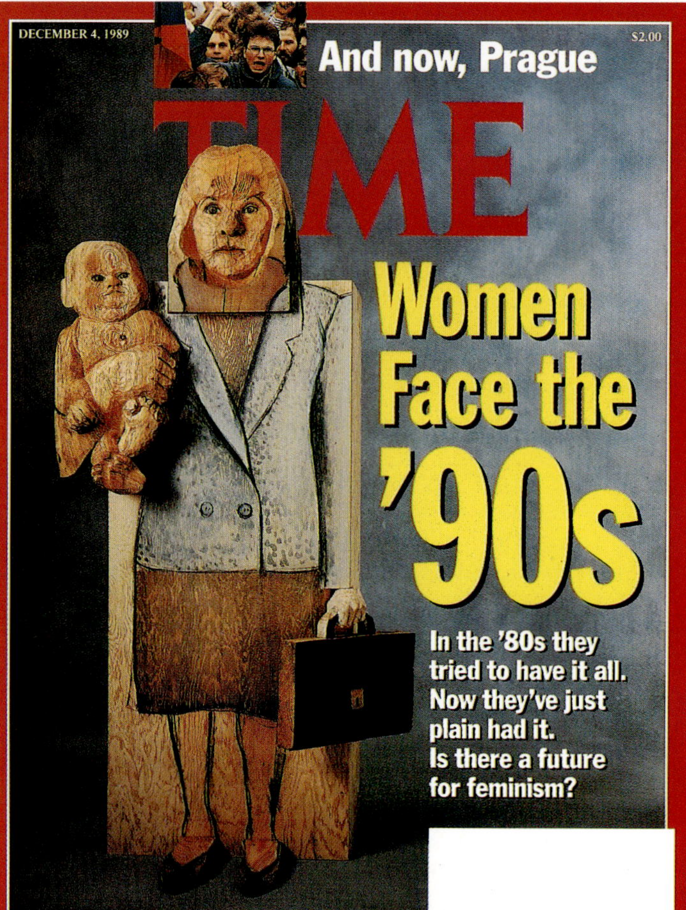

Women Face The 90's

3-D Illustrator: Marisol
Art Director: Rudolph C. Hoglund
Photographer: Roberto Brosan
Publisher: Time Warner, Inc.
Category: Consumer Magazine Cover

Best Of British

3-D Illustrator: Malcolm Fowler
Art Director: Tom Renolds
Photographer: Nancy Fouts
Agency: Shirt SleeVe Studio London
Publisher: Sunday Express Magazine
Client: Sunday Express Magazine
Category: Newspaper Sunday Supplement

NLJ/250

3-D Illustrator: Bonnie Rasmussen
Art Director: Doug Hunt
Photographer: Sauer & Associates/Paul B. Sauer
Agency: The National Law Journal
Publisher: The New York Law Publishing Company
Client: The National Law Journal
Category: Annual Report Cover

Perks That Work

3-D Illustrator: Joe Fleming
Art Director: Jackie Young
Photographer: See Spot Run
Agency: Ink Design
Publisher: Small Business Magazine
Category: Business Magazine Full Page

The Contortionist

3-D Illustrator: Walter Einsel
Art Director: Herb Rosenthal
Photographer: Walter Einsel
Client: P.T. Barnum Museum/Permanent Exhibit
Category: Miscellaneous

Heart

3-D Illustrator: Chuck Carlton
Art Director: Joe Boris
Photographer: Chuck Carlton/Chuck Pittman
Agency: 2217 A Studio
Category: Unpublished

Technology

3-D Illustrator: Joe Fleming
Art Director: Kathleen Hurd
Photographer: See Spot Run
Publisher: Inside Guide Magazine
Category: Editorial Illustration

28th Annual Outdoor Art Show

3-D Illustrator: Joe Fleming
Art Director: Paul Gilbert
Photographer: See Spot Run
Agency: Remarkable Communications
Client: Molson/City of Toronto
Category: Advertising Illustration

The extensive use of paper as a 3-D medium is quite evident. The quantity and quality of paper sculpture demonstrates its popularity as a viable 3-Dimensional Illustrative medium. Visual creatives are increasingly relying on paper sculpture to meet the requirements of an ever-changing industry. The techniques of curling, scoring and folding are used to create visually stimulating and technically demanding illustrations. Today, paper sculpture continues to spearhead the growth of 3-Dimensional Illustration and is an indispensable component of the industry.

ONLY LIFE
OFFERS MORE SUBTLETY.

HAMMERMILL.
MORE OF THE SUBTLETY
LIFE HAS TO OFFER.

Colors soft and warm. Textures gentle yet expressive, and inviting.

Hammermill Paper has captured nature's most elusive features to give your work the dignity and refinement it deserves.

Touch the velvety surface of this piece. That's our Vellum finish. It gives you the opacity and bulk of a textlike paper, without the textlike price. Our six other stock finishes are just as expressive.

Now look closely at the paper…it's Cream White. Perfect for attracting readers or viewers without distracting from your work.

There are 23 matching Hammermill Cover and Offset Opaque colors in all—plus White and Cream White. No other printing paper line gives you as broad a range of colors, stock sizes and weights to choose from.

Give your next printed piece the subtle difference it needs to stand apart.

Add life with Hammermill Papers.

HAMMERMILL
OFFSET OPAQUE®

This insert is printed by web offset on Hammermill Offset Opaque. Cream White. Substance 70. Vellum finish. Paper sculpture by Leo Monahan. © 1988 Hammermill Papers. Erie, PA 16533.

ONLY LIFE
OFFERS MORE VARIETY.
HAMMERMILL.
MORE OF THE VARIETY
LIFE HAS TO OFFER.
From the bold colors of an Indian headdress to the soft feel of a silk kimono, no one gives you as many ways to bring your work to life as Hammermill.
Look closely at the Lustre finish of this insert. Its smooth satin surface captures all the fragile detail of the artist's sculpture without the distracting glare of a glossy finish.
The bright white paper it's printed on works to enhance the detail and show Hammermill's other Cover colors at their fullest. There are 23 Hammermill Cover and Offset Opaque colors in all—plus White and Cream White.
If you'd like a closer look at just what Hammermill Papers can do for you, send for a free 17" x 22" poster of this insert.
Write on your company stationery to: Hammermill Papers, 6400 Poplar Avenue, Memphis, TN 38197-7000.
Choose the paper that gives you a range of possibilities. Add life with Hammermill Papers.
HAMMERMILL COVER
ONLY LIFE
OFFERS MORE CHARM.
HAMMERMILL.
MORE OF THE CHARM
LIFE HAS TO OFFER.
When it comes to delightful colors and textures, Hammermill Offset Opaque doesn't take a rumble seat to anybody.
The fact is, you can bet your Uncle Bob's brand new eight-button blazer and pearl-gray spats that no other printing paper gives you such a wide selection of colors and textures or such a broad range of stock sizes and weights. And no one tenders you these text-like features at such an un-text-like price.
That's what makes Offset Opaque the fashionable choice for everything from annual reports, booklets and brochures to portfolios, pamphlets and posters—and even magazine inserts.
Hammermill Offset Opaque comes in 23 captivating colors in all, plus White and Cream White—all with exactly matching Hammermill Cover colors. And in six distinctively different finishes, from super-smooth Lustre to the delicately textured Linen finish we've used for this insert. To send for a free 17" x 22" poster of this insert, write on your company stationery to: Hammermill Papers, 6400 Poplar Avenue, Memphis, Tennessee 38197-7000. Give your next printed piece a special brand of charm. Add life with Hammermill Papers.
HAMMERMILL OFFSET OPAQUE
INTERNATIONAL PAPER
ONLY LIFE
OFFERS MORE ELEGANCE.
HAMMERMILL.
MORE OF THE ELEGANCE
LIFE HAS TO OFFER.
Tall turreted castles and noble knights-errant are rich symbols of life in a more elegant age. It's that very sense of elegance which surfaces in a delicately embossed cover paper from Hammermill called Emissary.
The subtle yet distinctively different texture of this impressive sheet is as arresting to the touch as to the eye. And so, in a sense, it can make your art and messages doubly persuasive.
Emissary, like our seven other stock finishes, allows you to add text-like elegance and appeal to everything from annual reports and brochures to booklets and portfolios without paying a text-like price.
And it's available in both Hammermill Cover and Hammermill Offset Opaque in ten tempting colors. Plus Cream White and White.
For a closer look at just what Hammermill can do for you, send for a free 17" x 22" poster of this insert.
Write on your company stationery to: Hammermill Papers, 6400 Poplar Avenue, Memphis, Tennessee 38197-7000.
For your next printed piece, borrow a page from the age of elegance.
Add life with Hammermill Papers.
HAMMERMILL COVER
INTERNATIONAL PAPER

Siberian Tiger

3-D Illustrator: Meg White
Art Director: Meg White
Photographer: Chris Fieldhouse
Client: Meg White
Category: Unpublished

1889
1989

Milwaukee Repertory Theater

3-D Illustrator: Suzanne Moe-Duffeck
Art Director: Suzanne Moe-Duffeck
Photographer: Ferderbar Studios
Agency: Art Factory
Client: Milwaukee Repertory Theater

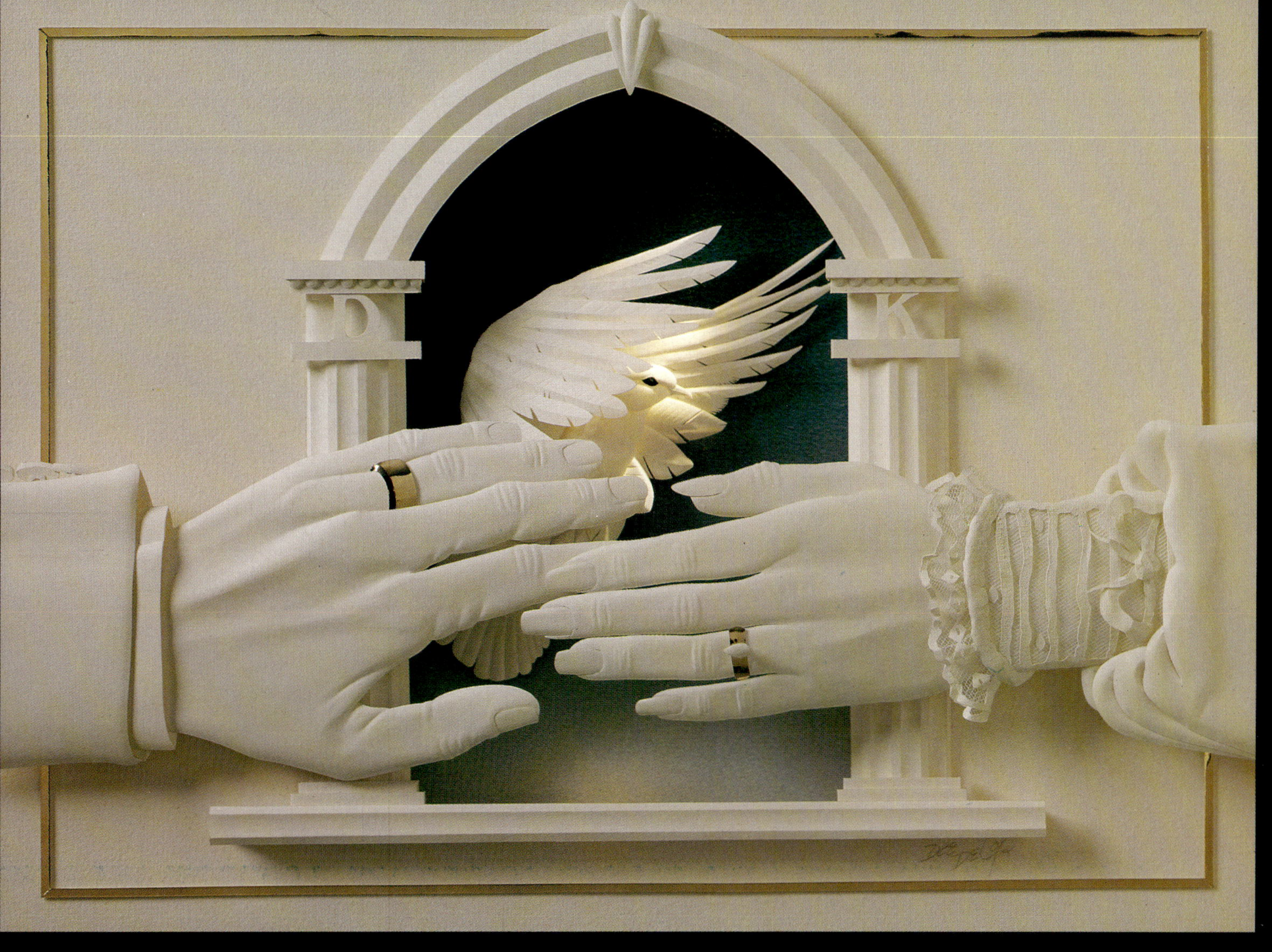

Wedding Hands

3-D Illustrator: Dee DeLoy
Art Director: Dee DeLoy
Photographer: Paul Gerding
Agency: Newstart Art
Client: Kathy DeLoy
Category: Wedding Invitation

Goldfish

3-D Illustrator: Joan Kritchman/Knuteson
Photographer: Joe Beauchamp/Summit Studio
Agency: Advertising Art Studios, Inc.
Category: Unpublished

Showcase

3-D Illustrator: Johnna Bandle
Art Director: Johnna Bandle
Photographer: Johnna Bandle
Publisher: American Showcase
Category: Advertising Illustration

Manpower Executive Calendar

3-D Illustrator: Johnna Bandle
Art Director: Brian Roach
Agency: Marcus Advertising
Client: Manpower
Category: Calendar

"Mallard"

April

s	m	t	w	t	f	s
1	2	3	4	5	6	7
8 *Palm Sunday*	9	10 *Passover Begins*	11	12	13 *Good Friday*	14
15 *Easter*	16	17	18	19	20	21
22	23	24	25	26	27	28
29	30					

MARCH

				1	2	3
4	5	6	7	8	9	10
11	12	13	14	15	16	17
18	19	20	21	22	23	24
25	26	27	28	29	30	31

MAY

		1	2	3	4	5
6	7	8	9	10	11	12
13	14	15	16	17	18	19
20	21	22	23	24	25	26
27	28	29	30	31		

Call Me Now Or The Sandwich Gets It!

3-D Illustrator: Hal Lōse

Is Your Pet Too Pudgy?

3-D Illustrator: Susan Ash
Art Director: Greg Kindred
Photographer: Steve Hix
Publisher: Veterinary Medicine Publishing
Client: Healthy Pet Magazine
Category: Consumer Magazine Cover

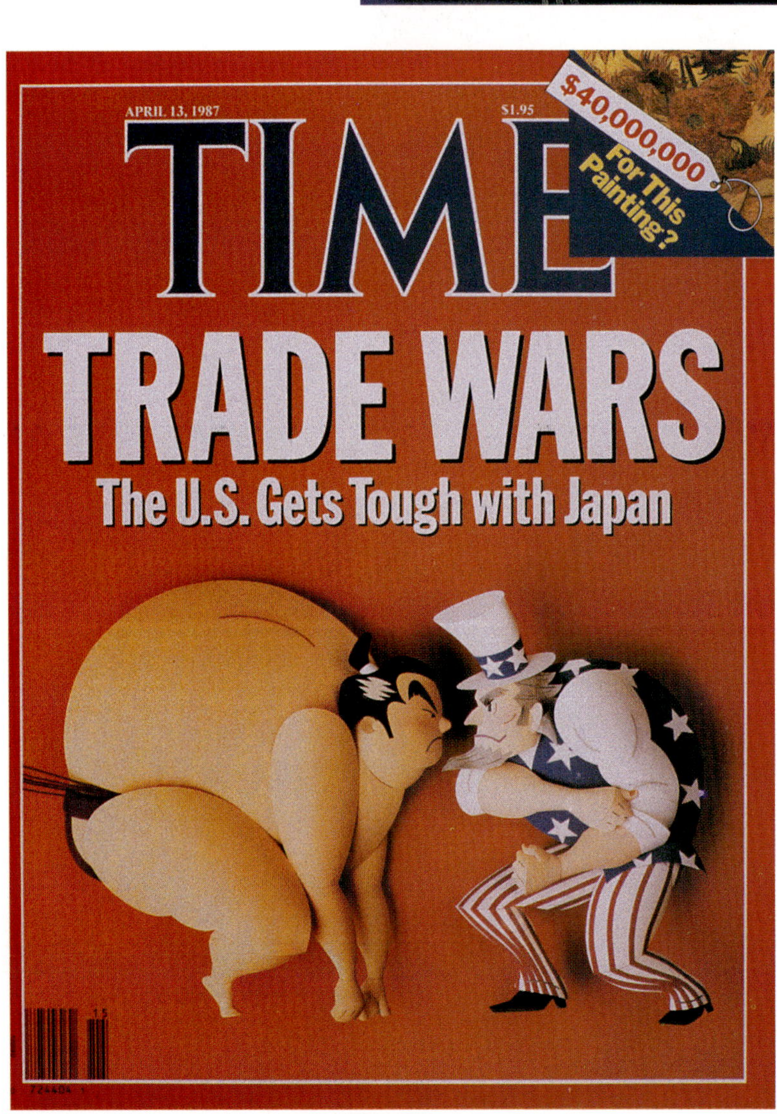

Trade Wars

3-D Illustrator: Ajin
Art Director: Rudolph C. Hoglund
Photographer: Tobe
Publisher: The Time Inc. Magazine Company
Client: Time Magazine
Category: Consumer Magazine Cover

Christian Classics

3-D Illustrator: Susan Ash
Art Director: Greg Breeding
Photographer: Ernie Block
Publisher: Worldwide Challenge
Client: Campus Crusade For Christ
Category: Consumer Magazine Campaign

NOW, I SAW IN MY DREAM that the highway up which Christian was to go was fenced on either side with a wall that was called Salvation (Isaiah 26:1). Up this way, therefore, did burdened Christian run, but not without great difficulty, because of the load on his back.

He ran thus till he came to a place somewhat ascending; and upon that place stood a cross, and a little below, in the bottom, a sepulchre. So I saw in my dream, that just as Christian came up with the cross, his burden loosed from off his shoulders and fell from off his back, and began to tumble, and so continued to do till it came to the mouth of the sepulchre, where it fell in, and I saw it no more.

When God releases us of our guilt and burden, we are as those that leap for joy.

Then was Christian glad and lightsome, and said with a merry heart, "He hath given me rest by His sorrow and life by His death." Then he stood still awhile to look and wonder; for it was very surprising to him that the sight of the cross should thus ease him of his burden. He looked, therefore, and looked again, even till the springs that were in his head sent the water down his cheeks (Zechariah 12:10).

Now, as he stood looking and weeping, behold, three Shining Ones came to him and saluted him with "Peace be to thee." So the first said to him, "Thy sins be forgiven thee" (Mark 2:5); the second stripped him of his rags and clothed him with a change of raiment (Zechariah 3:4); the third also set a mark on his forehead (Ephesians 1:13) and gave him a roll with a seal upon it, which he bade him look on as he ran, and that he should give it in at the celestial gate. So they went their way. Then Christian gave three leaps for joy and went on, singing:

"Thus far did I come laden with my sin;
Nor could aught ease the grief that I was in,
Till I came hither: what a place is this!
Must here be the beginning of my bliss?
Must here the burden fall from off my back?

Illustration by Susan Ash

Editor's note: The children, Peter, Susan, Lucy and Edmund, have just entered the land called Narnia through the wardrobe in the professor's house. Lucy, who had been to Narnia before and had been helped by a faun named Mr. Tumnus, discovers him missing from his forest home, taken into custody by the evil White Queen. The children find help in a kindly beaver couple. Here follows their conversation after dinner when Mr. Beaver has mentioned the powerful name: Aslan (the Christ figure).

"WHO IS ASLAN?" asked Susan.

"Aslan?" said Mr. Beaver, "Why, don't you know? He's the King. He's the Lord of the whole wood, but not often here, you understand. Never in my time or my father's time. But the word has reached us that he has come back. He is in Narnia at this moment. He'll settle the White Queen all right. It is he, not you, that will save Mr. Tumnus."

"She won't turn him into stone too?" said Edmund.

"Lord love you, Son of Adam, what a simple thing to say!" answered Mr. Beaver with a great laugh. "Turn *him* into stone? If she can stand on her two feet and look him in the face, it'll be the most she can do and more than I expect of her. No, no. He'll put all to rights as it says in an old rhyme in these parts:

Wrong will be right, when Aslan comes in sight,
At the sound of his roar, sorrows will be no more,
When he bares his teeth, winter meets its death
And when he shakes his mane, we shall have spring again.

You'll understand when you see him."

"But shall we see him?" asked Susan.

"Why, Daughter of Eve, that's what I brought you here for. I'm to lead you where you shall meet him," said Mr. Beaver.

"Is—is he a man?" asked Lucy.

"Aslan a man!" said Mr. Beaver sternly. "Certainly not. I tell you he is the King of the wood and the son of the great Emperor-Beyond-the-Sea. Don't you know who is the King of Beasts? Aslan is a lion—*the* Lion, the great Lion."

"Ooh!" said Susan, "I'd thought he was a man. Is he—quite safe? I shall feel rather nervous about meeting a lion."

"That you will, dearie, and no mistake," said Mrs. Beaver. "If there's anyone who can appear before Aslan without his knees knocking, he's either braver than most or else just silly."

"Then he isn't safe?" said Lucy.

"Safe?" said Mr. Beaver. "Don't you hear what Mrs. Beaver tells you? Who said anything about safe? 'Course he isn't safe. But he's good. He's the King, I tell you."

Illustration by Susan Ash

HAS IT EVER OCCURRED to you that the design of prayer in the divine economy is a fantastically puzzling mystery? Why should there be a system or plan of prayer at all? Self-sufficiency is one of the attributes of God. Could not He who spoke the worlds into existence and who upholds them by that same Word accomplish His purposes without the help of puny man? Then why did He devise the plan of prayer?

The mystery of the design of prayer is pointed up in Ezekiel 22:30-31. During a time of national apostasy, God said, "And I sought for a man among them, that should make up the hedge, and stand in the gap before Me for the land, that I should not destroy it; but I found none. Therefore have I poured out Mine indignation upon them; I have consumed them with the fire of My wrath; and their own way have I recompensed upon their heads."

Here we see God seeking to avoid exercising just and deserved judgment. He, Himself, longs to spare the nation. But, strangely, He is "helpless" without a man, without an intercessor. Why did He set up a system that made Him "dependent" upon a man?

That He will do nothing in the realm of human redemption, since its inception, outside of this scheme of prayer and intercession is indicated by God's many pressing invitations to prayer in His Word. One translator has paraphrased Matthew 7:7 thus: "Ask, I ask you to ask; seek, I entreat you to seek; knock, I urge you to knock."

He not only invites and exhorts us to pray, He also commands: "Pray ye, therefore, the Lord of the harvest, that He will send forth laborers into His harvest" (Matthew 9:38). He is Himself the Lord of the harvest. The harvest is His. The laborers are His. Why should He stand "helplessly" by while urging men to pray reapers into the fields? Why does He send forth laborers only in answer to the prayers of the redeemed?

The fundamental importance of this scheme of prayer in God's economy is further emphasized by God's binding Himself unequivocally

Illustration by Susan Ash

Pros And Cons Of State Licensure

3-D Illustrator: Leo Monahan
Art Director: Kathleen Cuddihy
Photographer: Stephen E. Munz
Publisher: Medical Economics Company
Client: MLO
Category: Business Magazine Cover

Super Joe

3-D Illustrator: Bill Miller
Art Director: Geoffrey Shives
Photographer: Bill Miller
Publisher: Advertising Age
Client: Crains Chicago Business News
Category: Business Magazine Cover

Here They Come

3-D Illustrator: Andrew Nitzberg
Art Director: Ed Rosanio
Photographer: Gary Donnelly
Publisher: Springhouse Corporation
Client: Learning Magazine
Category: Business Magazine Cover

Medication Errors

3-D Illustrator: Andrew Nitzberg
Art Director: Ed Rosanio
Photographer: Gary Donnelly
Publisher: Springhouse Corporation
Client: Nursing Magazine
Category: Business Magazine Spread

SCULPTURE BY ANDREW NITZBERG/PHOTOGRAPH BY GARY DONNELLY

NEW STRATEGIES FOR AVOIDING

MEDICATION ERRORS

Complications...increased costs ...lawsuits. Nurses and pharmacists alike know the high price of medication errors. Unfortunately, errors do occur, despite everyone's best efforts to eliminate them. But by taking advantage of strategies designed to reduce administration errors, we can work together to minimize risks.

In this article, I'll discuss some of the most effective approaches available today. To reduce errors on your unit, you may want to ask your nursing practice committee to consider some of them.

Unit-dose packaging

One of the first strategies designed to reduce medication errors was the unit-dose system. With a centralized system, all drug orders are processed in the main pharmacy. Here's a common protocol:

- The pharmacy receives a copy of each doctor's orders.
- In the pharmacy, which maintains medication profiles on all patients, each medication order is entered into the correct profile.
- Before dispensing a new drug, the pharmacist checks the administration time and route and compares the order with other current drug orders for potential problems such as allergic reactions, interactions, or duplicate therapy.
- The pharmacist dispenses the drug in a unit-dose package, which contains the ordered dose in a form ready for administration. The drug is labeled with the drug name, dose, instructions for preparation, lot number, and expiration date.
- Drugs for each patient are dispensed

For a fresh look at ways to reduce dangerous drug administration errors, consider these innovative approaches.

BY DONNA S. CARR, PharmD
Assistant Professor, Pharmacy Practice
University of South Carolina College of Pharmacy
Columbia, South Carolina

Nursing89, August 39

Put Electricity To Your Coffee

3-D Illustrator: Søren Thaee
Art Director: Søren Thaee
Photographer: Planet Foto
Publisher: Elnyt
Client: Elnyt
Category: Consumer Magazine Cover

A Visit To Denmark's New Planetarium

3-D Illustrator: Søren Thaae
Photographer: Planet Foto
Publisher: Elnyt
Client: Elnyt
Category: Consumer Magazine Cover

The Last Lighthouse Ship

3-D Illustrator: Søren Thaae
Photographer: Planet Foto
Publisher: Elnyt
Client: Elnyt
Category: Consumer Magazine Cover

Far Eastern Travel

3-D Illustrator: Sally Vitsky
Art Director: Stanley Braverman
Photographer: David Spindel
Publisher: American Express
Client: Signature Magazine
Category: Consumer Magazine Cover

Fluoridation/Health Measure Or Hoax

3-D Illustrator: Toby Williams
Art Director: Betsy Woldman
Photographer: Ed Slaman
Publisher: East/West Journal
Client: East/West Journal
Category: Consumer Magazine Full Page

Business & Computer Papers

3-D Illustrator: Joseph DeCerchio
Art Director: Dave Beverage
Photographer: Bill Kovnat
Publisher: Springhouse Corporation
Client: Office Systems
Category: Business Magazine Spread

Home Mission

3-D Illustrator: Søren Thaae
Art Director: Søren Thaae
Photographer: Charly Fotograph
Publisher: Lohses Forlag
Client: The Home Mission
Category: Advertising Direct Mail Poster

Note Cube Portfolio

3-D Illustrator: Pat Allen
Art Director: Bill Whiddon
Photographer: Jim Scherzi
Agency: Colburn Whiddon Advertising, Inc.
Client: International Note Cube Corporation
Category: Advertising Direct Mail Brochure

Skiers Vacation

3-D Illustrator: Dee DeLoy
Art Director: Nigel Fulleck
Photographer: Paul Gerding
Agency: Newstart Art
Publisher: RMS Tours
Client: RMS Tours
Category: Advertising Direct Mail Brochure

Ramases II Exhibit

3-D Illustrator: Sally Vitsky
Art Director: Paul Rousso
Photographer: Lee Salsbery
Agency: Shotwell & Partners
Client: Charlotte-North Carolina
Category: Advertising Direct Mail Brochure

Good Health

3-D Illustrator: George Suyeoka
Art Director: Angela Perez
Photographer: Ralph Cowan
Agency: George Suyeoka
Publisher: Baxter Lab
Client: Baxter Lab
Category: Advertising Direct Mail Poster

G.E. Past To Present

3-D Illustrator: Meg White
Art Director: Laura Robinson
Photographer: Don Burton
Agency: Power Graphics
Client: G.E. Edison Club
Category: Annual Report Cover

Aloha

3-D Illustrator: Chuck Sisson
Art Director: Chuck Sisson
Photographer: Gary Bartholomew
Copywriter: Faith Watson
Agency: Jane Szabo Design Associates
Publisher: RPP Enterprises
Client: Motorola Cellular Subscriber Division
Category: Advertising Direct Mail Business Brochure

Maui is the second largest island in Hawaii's chain. Its existence began as two volcanic land masses, which were eventually joined by their own lava flows (hence its nickname, the Valley Island).

Maui, the Valley Island, has a slogan: "Maui no ke oi" (Maui is the greatest).

HEMOLELE MOKUPUNI...(Perfect Island)

And then there's the weather. Undeniably the best in the country, arguably, the best in the world. Its perfection is credited both to the position of the islands in the ocean and the northeast tradewinds. Either way, even the rain is beautiful on Maui!

MOMONA MAKANA...(Rich Reward)

1988 marked the beginning of a new era for Motorola's Cellular Sales force; an era of achievement, honor and recognition. This tradition of superior accomplishment continues in 1989.

Consider the prestige of meeting the high standards of success necessary to become a Signal Society member. Consider, too, the surf, sand and sun this year's Signal Elite group will enjoy on magnificent Maui.

To pay tribute to an outstanding year-long effort, we will honor Signal Elite members at a fabulous awards banquet at the Maui Inter Continental Wailea, which will also serve as our headquarters during the week long utopian holiday. In addition, Society rings of black onyx and gold will be presented, their design as distinctive as the achievement they represent.

Also recognized will be those who attain the Signal Society's second level of excellence, the Pacesetters. These ambitious go-getters will attend a special awards banquet of their own in Chicago, where they will receive a striking gold Signal Society lapel pin.

From January 1, 1989 through December 31, 1989, we will track direct and indirect sales people based on Official Program Rules, looking for leaders from around the country. Set your sights high... rich rewards can be yours!

The magic of Maui is inescapable. It's a place where visitors are dazzled by luxurious accommodations and splendid shopping, enchanted by a remarkable ancient history and charmed by glimpses of frontier roots in the days of the wild west.

Add to all this an abundance of natural and historic landmarks, a heavy dose of native culture (hula lessons are a must), and picture postcard flora and fauna.

This year Signal Society members will have a chance to investigate that local claim for themselves.

One trait that characterizes the people of Maui is the "Spirit of Aloha"—a genuine friendliness, a willingness to give freely.

In this spirit, Motorola presents the Cellular Sales organization with an opportunity to set and reach a most worthwhile goal in 1989. The Signal Society awaits ...and so does the Valley Island.

We Get Denmark Growing

3-D Illustrator: Søren Thaae
Art Director: Henning Lorup
Photographer: Charly Fotograph
Agency: Dot Zero
Client: Superfos Korn
Category: Advertising Poster Campaign

Integrated Business Solutions

3-D Illustrator: Vladimir Paperny
Art Director: Tom Bant
Photographer: Vladimir Paperny
Agency: Electro Ad Agency
Client: Time Electronics
Category: Advertising Direct Mail Brochure

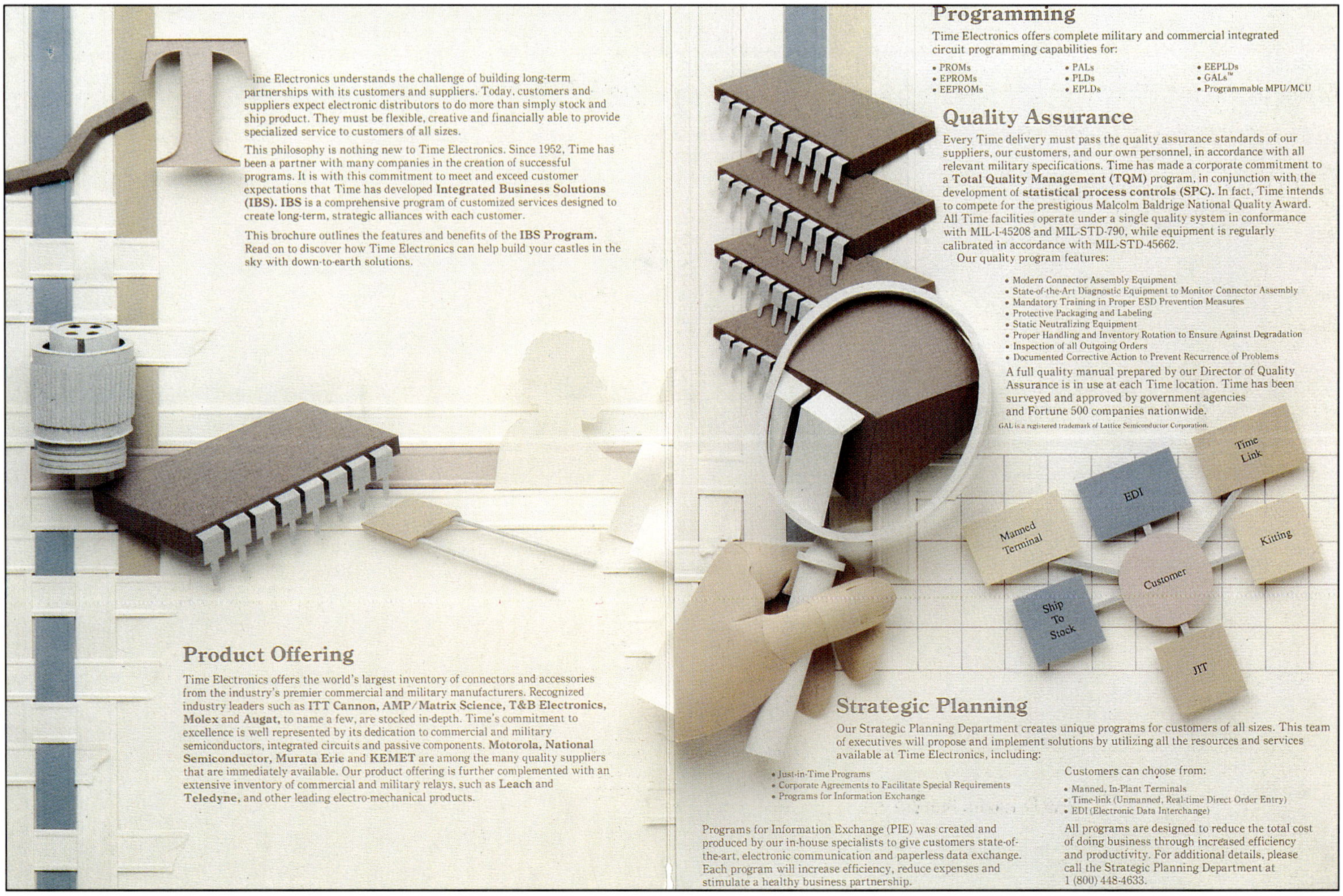

Time Electronics understands the challenge of building long-term partnerships with its customers and suppliers. Today, customers and suppliers expect electronic distributors to do more than simply stock and ship product. They must be flexible, creative and financially able to provide specialized service to customers of all sizes.

This philosophy is nothing new to Time Electronics. Since 1952, Time has been a partner with many companies in the creation of successful programs. It is with this commitment to meet and exceed customer expectations that Time has developed **Integrated Business Solutions (IBS). IBS** is a comprehensive program of customized services designed to create long-term, strategic alliances with each customer.

This brochure outlines the features and benefits of the **IBS Program.** Read on to discover how Time Electronics can help build your castles in the sky with down-to-earth solutions.

Product Offering

Time Electronics offers the world's largest inventory of connectors and accessories from the industry's premier commercial and military manufacturers. Recognized industry leaders such as **ITT Cannon, AMP/Matrix Science, T&B Electronics, Molex** and **Augat,** to name a few, are stocked in-depth. Time's commitment to excellence is well represented by its dedication to commercial and military semiconductors, integrated circuits and passive components. **Motorola, National Semiconductor, Murata Erie** and **KEMET** are among the many quality suppliers that are immediately available. Our product offering is further complemented with an extensive inventory of commercial and military relays, such as **Leach** and **Teledyne,** and other leading electro-mechanical products.

Programming

Time Electronics offers complete military and commercial integrated circuit programming capabilities for:

- PROMs
- EPROMs
- EEPROMs
- PALs
- PLDs
- EPLDs
- EEPLDs
- GALs™
- Programmable MPU/MCU

Quality Assurance

Every Time delivery must pass the quality assurance standards of our suppliers, our customers, and our own personnel, in accordance with all relevant military specifications. Time has made a corporate commitment to a **Total Quality Management (TQM)** program, in conjunction with the development of **statistical process controls (SPC).** In fact, Time intends to compete for the prestigious Malcolm Baldrige National Quality Award. All Time facilities operate under a single quality system in conformance with MIL-I-45208 and MIL-STD-790, while equipment is regularly calibrated in accordance with MIL-STD-45662.

Our quality program features:

- Modern Connector Assembly Equipment
- State-of-the-Art Diagnostic Equipment to Monitor Connector Assembly
- Mandatory Training in Proper ESD Prevention Measures
- Protective Packaging and Labeling
- Static Neutralizing Equipment
- Proper Handling and Inventory Rotation to Ensure Against Degradation
- Inspection of all Outgoing Orders
- Documented Corrective Action to Prevent Recurrence of Problems

A full quality manual prepared by our Director of Quality Assurance is in use at each Time location. Time has been surveyed and approved by government agencies and Fortune 500 companies nationwide.

GAL is a registered trademark of Lattice Semiconductor Corporation.

Time Link
EDI
Manned Terminal
Kitting
Customer
Ship To Stock
JIT

Strategic Planning

Our Strategic Planning Department creates unique programs for customers of all sizes. This team of executives will propose and implement solutions by utilizing all the resources and services available at Time Electronics, including:

- Just-in-Time Programs
- Corporate Agreements to Facilitate Special Requirements
- Programs for Information Exchange

Programs for Information Exchange (PIE) was created and produced by our in-house specialists to give customers state-of-the-art, electronic communication and paperless data exchange. Each program will increase efficiency, reduce expenses and stimulate a healthy business partnership.

Customers can choose from:

- Manned, In-Plant Terminals
- Time-link (Unmanned, Real-time Direct Order Entry)
- EDI (Electronic Data Interchange)

All programs are designed to reduce the total cost of doing business through increased efficiency and productivity. For additional details, please call the Strategic Planning Department at 1 (800) 448-4633.

Hawaii "The Power Within"

3-D Illustrator: Cindy Berglund
Art Director: Mike Thomas
Photographer: Rod Pierce
Agency: Carlson Companies, Inc./Berglund Design
Publisher: Carlson Companies, Inc.
Client: Northern Telecom
Category: Advertising Direct Mail Poster

We Network People

3-D Illustrator: Phyllis Luch
Art Director: Grant Phelps
Photographer: Michael McRae
Agency: Hurst & Phillips
Publisher: MacWorld
Client: Dayna
Category: Advertising Spread

Party With The Parrot

3-D Illustrator: Cindy Berglund
Art Director: Jon Trettel
Photographer: Rod Pierce
Agency: Kroese & Heffelfinger
Cindy Berglund Illustration & Design
Publisher: Kroese & Heffelfinger
Client: Phillips Products Company
Category: Advertising Direct Mail Consumer Campaign

PARTY WITH THE PARROT
READY TO DRINK
EL LORO™ BRAND MARGARITAS
Original, Peach and Raspberry

Autumn Hunt

3-D Illustrator: Cindy Berglund
Art Director: Leone Medin
Photographer: Rod Pierce
Agency: Cindy Berglund Illustration & Design
Publisher: Radisson Hotels International
Client: Radisson Hotels International
Category: Advertising Direct Mail Consumer Poster

Travel The USA

3-D Illustrator: Gus Alavezos
Art Director: James Faye
Photographer: Kevin Saehlenou
Agency: Graphics Group
Client: Holiday Rambler/RV's Camper
Category: Advertising Consumer Magazine Spread

Effervescent Tablets

3-D Illustrator: Johnna Bandle
Photographer: Johnna Bandle
Agency: Johnson & Dean
Client: Perrigo Company
Category: Advertising Consumer Magazine Full Page

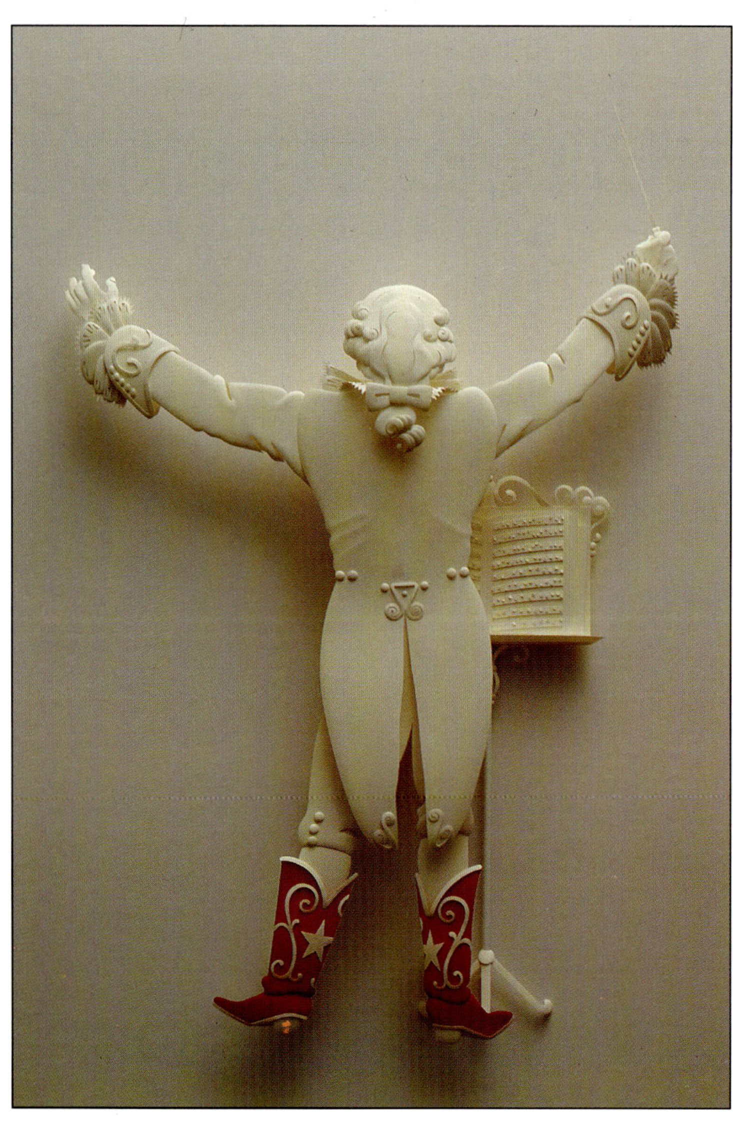

Mozart In Red Boots

3-D Illustrator: Johnna Bandle
Photographer: Johnna Bandle
Client: Dallas Symphony
Category: Advertising Direct Mail Poster

Zoomobile

3-D Illustrator: Susan Ash
Art Director: Susan Ash
Photographer: David Ludwigs
Agency: Bernstein Rein Advertising
Client: McDonald's/Henry Doorly Zoo
Category: Advertising Direct Mail Poster

Piñata

3-D Illustrator: Gus Alavezos
Art Director: Lindsay Hanson
Photographer: Kevin Saehlenou
Agency: Evan's Phoenix
Client: Garcia's
Category: Advertising Direct Mail Poster

$10,000.00
SCHOLARSHIP
USE YOUR NOODLE SWEEPSTAKES
NISSIN
GRAND PRIZE
$10,000 Scholarship in U.S. Savings Bonds
5 SECOND PRIZES
$2,500 Scholarship in U.S. Savings Bonds
25 THIRD PRIZES
A year's supply of
NISSIN
Cup O' Noodles
The Perfect After School Snack
ENTER TODAY AND WIN
NO PURCHASE NECESSARY
NISSIN
Cup O' Noodles
MUCH MORE THAN A SOUP

WINTER WARE
from
NISSIN
Top Ramen.
FREE Winter Ware from TOP RAMEN, the authentic oriental noodle soup. This authentic oriental noodle bowl, imported from Japan and made of stoneware, can be yours FREE—with UPC symbols from any of the delicious flavors of TOP RAMEN. This exclusively designed bowl is microwaveable, dishwasher safe, and the ideal serving size for TOP RAMEN, America's favorite oriental noodle soup. So start saving your TOP RAMEN UPC symbols and send for your FREE, authentic oriental noodle bowl with the order form below. Hurry, supplies are limited.
NISSIN
Top Ramen

Cup O'Noodles

3-D Illustrator: Jeff Nishinaka
Art Director: Sachi Kuwahara
Photographer: Ed Ikuta
Agency: Sawcheese Studio
Client: Nissin Foods
Category: Miscellaneous

90 Minutes 'Til Lift-Off

3-D Illustrator: Jeff Nishinaka
Art Director: Greg Nygard
Photographer: Ed Ikuta
Agency: Zechman & Associates
Client: Cheeca Lodge
Category: Miscellaneous

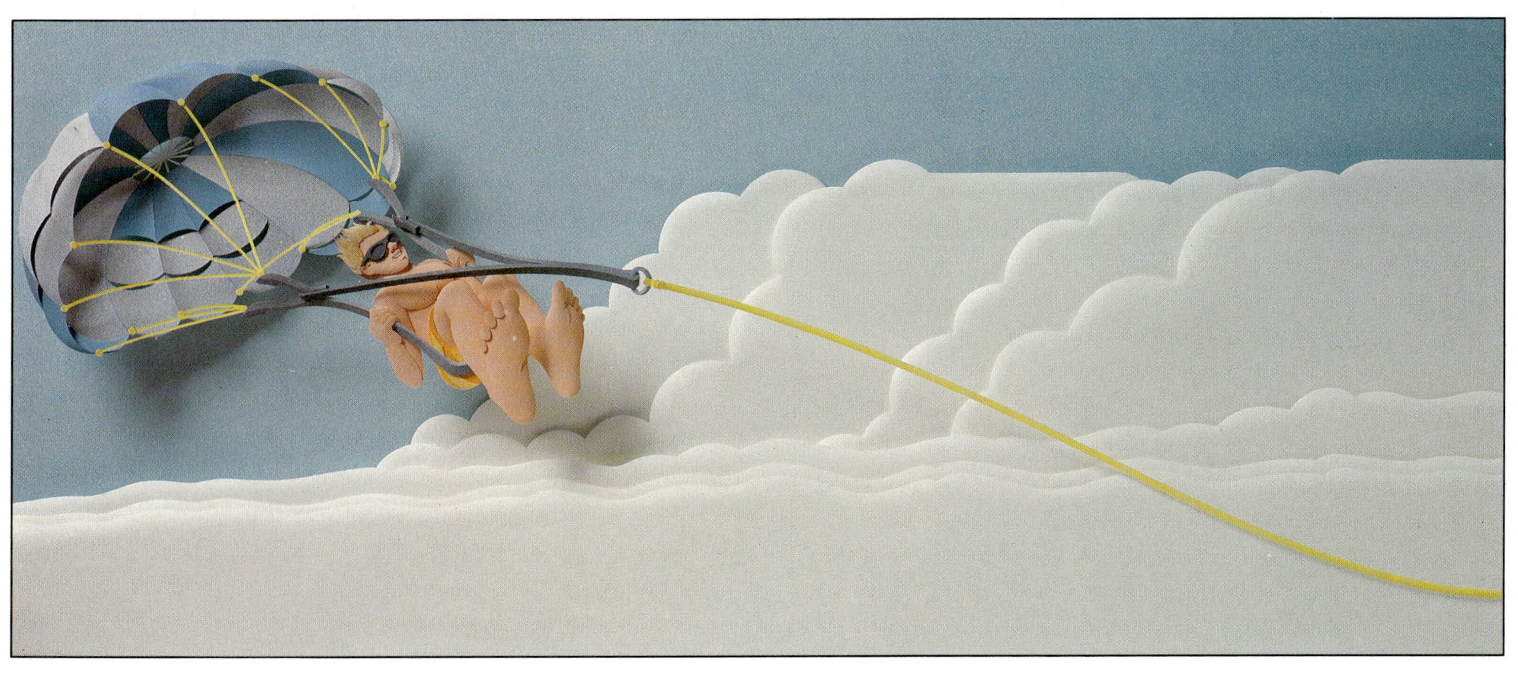

The World Theater

3-D Illustrator: Cindy Berglund
Art Director: John Pearson
Photographer: Rod Pierce
Agency: Cindy Berglund Illustration & Design
Publisher: Minnesota Public Radio
Client: The World Theater
Category: Advertising Illustration

North Ridge Point

3-D Illustrator: Johnna Bandle
Art Director: Linda Cogswell
Photographer: Johnna Bandle
Client: North Ridge Point
Category: Advertising Illustration

Cover H&R Block

3-D Illustrator: Johnna Bandle
Art Director: Dwight Widaman
Photographer: Johnna Bandle
Client: H&R Block
Category: Editorial Illustration

By The Sea

3-D Illustrator: Eileen Hahn
Category: Unpublished

Gossip

3-D Illustrator: Paige Billin-Frye
Art Director: Lauren Klementz-Harte/Paige Billin-Frye
Photographer: Steve Weber
Client: Paige Billin-Frye
Category: Self-Promotion Flyer

Oasis

3-D Illustrator: Marilyn Bass
Art Director: Chel Dong
Photographer: Marvin Goldman
Agency: Bass & Goldman
Publisher: Institutional Investor
Client: Institutional Investor
Category: Editorial Illustration

His 'N' Hers

3-D Illustrator: Paige Billin-Frye
Art Director: The Illustrators Workshop
Photographer: Adam Koons
Agency: The Illustrators Workshop
Category: Self Promotion Flyer

It's The Real Thing

3-D Illustrator: Gus Alavezos
Photographer: Kevin Saehlenou
Category: Unpublished

New Africa II

3-D Illustrator: Mark Falls
Art Director: Mark Falls
Photographer: Chuck Carlton
Agency: Mark Falls Studio
Publisher: Celluloid Records
Client: Celluloid Records
Category: Record Cover

Santa

3-D Illustrator: Johnna Bandle
Art Director: Joseph Wisniewski
Photographer: Johnna Bandle
Client: J.C. Penny
Category: Newspaper Sunday Supplement

Tree With Square Roots

3-D Illustrator: Bill Finewood
Photographer: Bill Finewood
Publisher: Silver, Burdett & Ginn
Category: Textbook

French Hen

3-D Illustrator: Bill Finewood
Art Director: Linda Oreman
Photographer: Bill Finewood
Agency: Art Works, Inc.
Publisher: Linda Oreman Artists Rep
Category: Self Promotion Poster

The Good Samaritan

3-D Illustrator: Hal Lōse
Art Director: Hal Lōse
Photographer: Howard Gale
Client: The Lutheran Church of America
Category: Editorial Illustration

This Is Relaxing?

3-D Illustrator: Jack Graham
Art Director: Curtis Carter
Photographer: Bob Carey
Publisher: George Gretser
Client: Private Clubs Magazine
Category: Editorial Illustration

It's Not Too Late

3-D Illustrator: Phyllis Luch
Art Director: Warren Luch
Photographer: Steve Tregeagle
Publisher: L.D.S. Church
Category: Editorial Illustration

Marbled Lai

3-D Illustrator: Hal Lōse
Art Director: Hal Lōse
Photographer: Howard Gale
Agency: Graphic Decisions
Client: RCA/GE
Category: Advertising Illustration

Birthday Card/Wreath With Birds

3-D Illustrator: Johnna Bandle
Art Director: Steve Hess
Client: Hallmark Cards, Inc.
Category: Greeting Card

Mother's Day Card/Lilies

3-D Illustrator: Johnna Bandle
Art Director: Tammy Palm
Client: Ambassador Cards
Category: Greeting Card

Happy Valentine's Day Mom

3-D Illustrator: Johnna Bandle
Photographer: Johnna Bandle
Client: Hallmark Cards, Inc.
Category: Greeting Card

Victorian Rose

3-D Illustrator: Cindy Berglund
Art Director: Mary Owen
Photographer: Rod Pierce
Agency: Cindy Berglund Illustration & Design
Client: Deluxe Corporation
Category: Unpublished

August

s	m	t	w	t	f	s
			1	2	3	4
5	6	7	8	9	10	11
12	13	14	15	16	17	18
19	20	21	22	23	24	25
26	27	28	29	30	31	

Helianthus

3-D Illustrator: Jerry Pavey
Art Director: Jerry Pavey
Photographer: Tom Radcliffe
Agency: Jerry Pavey Design & Illustration
Publisher: S&S Graphics, Inc.
Client: S.D. Warren Paper Company/S&S Graphics, Inc.
Category: Calendar Full Page

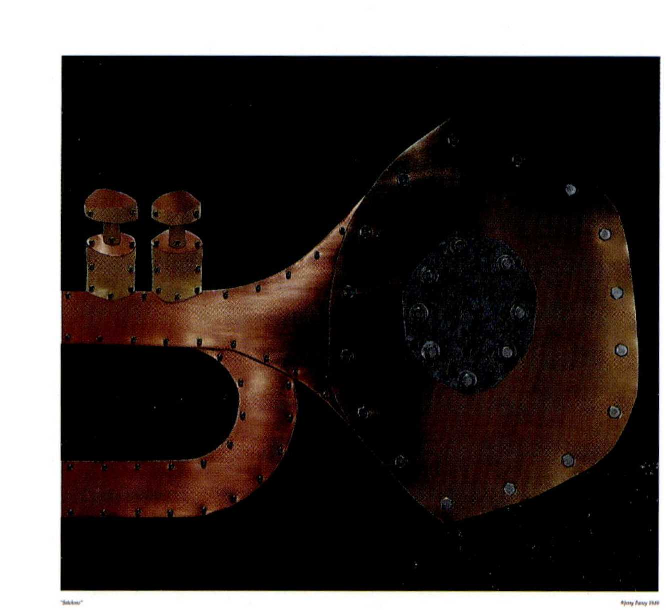

January

s	m	t	w	t	f	s
	1 New Year's Day	2	3	4	5	6
7	8	9	10	11	12	13
14	15 Martin Luther King Day	16	17	18	19	20
21	22	23	24	25	26	27
28	29	30	31			

Satchmo

3-D Illustrator: Jerry Pavey
Art Director: Jerry Pavey
Photographer: William McCaw
Agency: Jerry Pavey Design & Illustration
Publisher: S&S Graphics, Inc
Client: S.D. Warren Paper Company/S&S Graphics, Inc.
Category: Calendar Full Page

Campbell Kid Calendar

3-D Illustrator: Lisa Tysko
Art Director: Lisa Tysko
Photographer: Michael Berry
Agency: 361 Design Group
Client: Campbell Soup Company
Category: Complete Calendar

Easter Seal

3-D Illustrator: Cindy Berglund
Art Director: Scott Kirkpatrick
Photographer: Steve Umland
Agency: Campbell-Mithun-Esty, Inc.
Publisher: National Easter Seal Society
Client: National Easter Seal Society
Category: Postage Stamp

Remembering Norman Rockwell

3-D Illustrator: Bill Miller
Art Director: Bob Bowmen
Photographer: Ron Gould
Client: Bradford Exchange
Category: Miscellaneous

Pepsi P.O.P.

3-D Illustrator: Tak Murakami
Art Director: Charles Willard
Photographer: Tak Murakami
Client: Tracy-Locke Agency/Dallas Texas
Category: Advertising Point of Purchase

Vladimir Paperny
& Associates
Coast-To-Coast
Creative
Services
1114 Twelfth St.
Suite 101
Santa Monica
California 90403
(213) 393-7564

Stationery Set

3-D Illustrator: Vladimir Paperny
Art Director: Vladimir Paperny
Photographer: Vladimir Paperny
Agency: Vladimir Paperny & Associates
Client: Vladimir Paperny & Associates
Category: Self Promotion Stationery

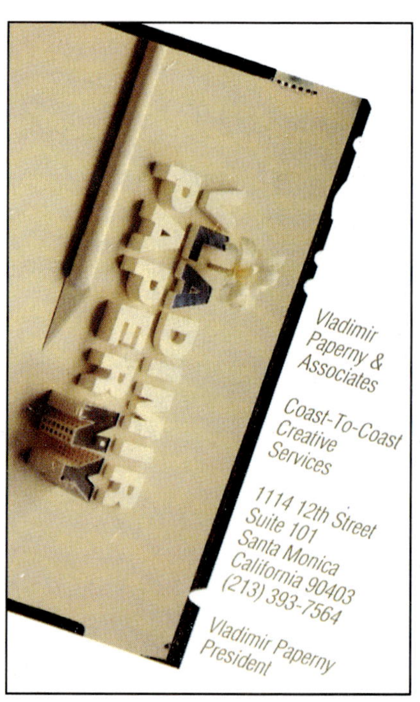

South American Cooking

3-D Illustrator: Lisa Tysko
Art Director: Lisa Tysko
Photographer: Michael Berry
Agency: 361 Design Group
Client: 361 Design Group
Category: Self Promotion Flyer

P A P E R S C U L P T U R E

LISA TYSKO

THREE-SIX-ONE DESIGN GROUP, 361 NASSAU STREET, PRINCETON, NJ 08540
TEL: (609) 921-3610 / FAX: (609) 921-8235

Talking Heads

3-D Illustrator: Jerry Cable
Art Director: Jerry Cable
Photographer: Ron Scalera
Client: Jerry Cable Design
Category: Self Promotion Flyer

Jerry Cable
DESIGN
133 KUHL ROAD
FLEMINGTON
NEW JERSEY
08822

STUDIO & FAX PHONE
201-788-8673

Visual Communication with an Accent on Design

If You Want To Get Ahead

Try One of Mine

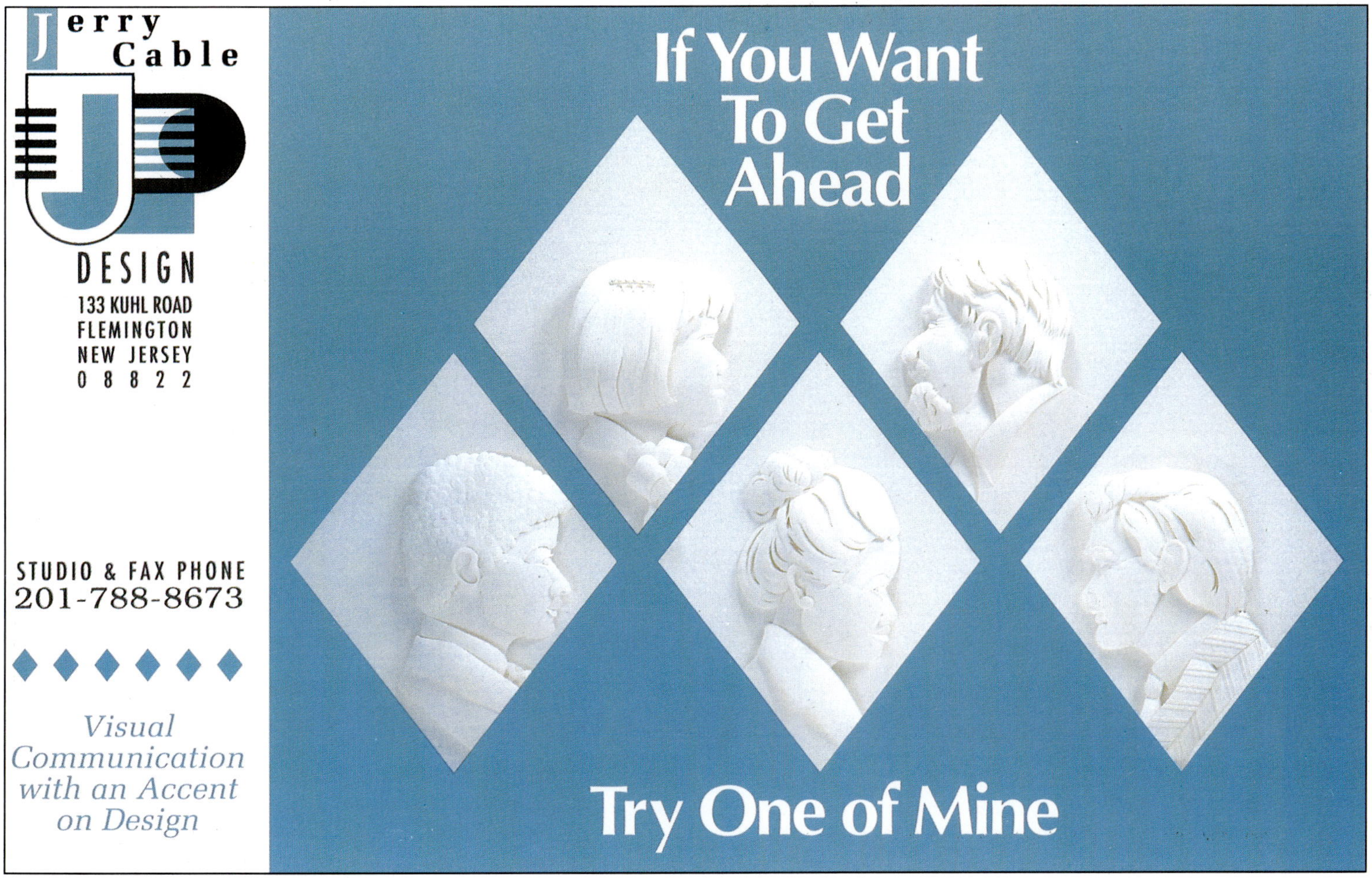

Cindy Berglund Represented by Sandra Heinen (612) 332-3671

Self Promotion

3-D Illustrator: Cindy Berglund
Art Director: Sandra Heinen
Photographer: Mark LaFavor/Jim Battis
Agency: Cindy Berglund Illustration & Design
Publisher: Heinen & Company
Client: Cindy Berglund Illustration & Design
Heinen & Company
Category: Self Promotion Flyer

The SCHUNA GROUP
700 SO. 3RD ST., #301 MPLS., MN 55415

Cindy Berglund is represented by JoAnne Schuna (612)343-0432; Frank Schuna (612)343-0104

Chart Your Course!

3-D Illustrator: Cindy Berglund
Art Director: JoAnne Schuna
Photographer: Mark LaFavor
Agency: The Schuna Group
Publisher: The Schuna Group
Client: Cindy Berglund/The Schuna Group
Category: Self Promotion Flyer

Self Promotion

3-D Illustrator: Sally Vitsky
Art Director: Sally Vitsky
Photographer: Lee Salsbery
Client: Sally Vitsky
Category: Self Promotion

Louie Armstrong

3-D Illustrator: Johnna Bandle
Art Director: Johnna Bandle
Photographer: Johnna Bandle
Publisher: American Showcase
Category: Self Promotion

Dancing Couple

3-D Illustrator: Gus Alavezos
Photographer: Kevin Saehlenou
Category: Unpublished

Carousel

3-D Illustrator: Joseph DeCerchio
Art Director: Joseph DeCerchio
Photographer: Bill Kovnat
Client: JDC Designs
Category: Self Promotion Postcard

Glowing Man

3-D Illustrator: Meg White
Art Director: Kevin Darst
Photographer: Geoff Carr
Agency: KDEE, Inc.
Client: Meg White
Category: Unpublished

David Letterman

3-D Illustrator: Meg White
Art Director: Meg White
Photographer: Geoff Carr
Client: Meg White
Category: Unpublished

Night

3-D Illustrator: Kinley W. Borden
Art Director: Kinley W. Borden
Category: Unpublished

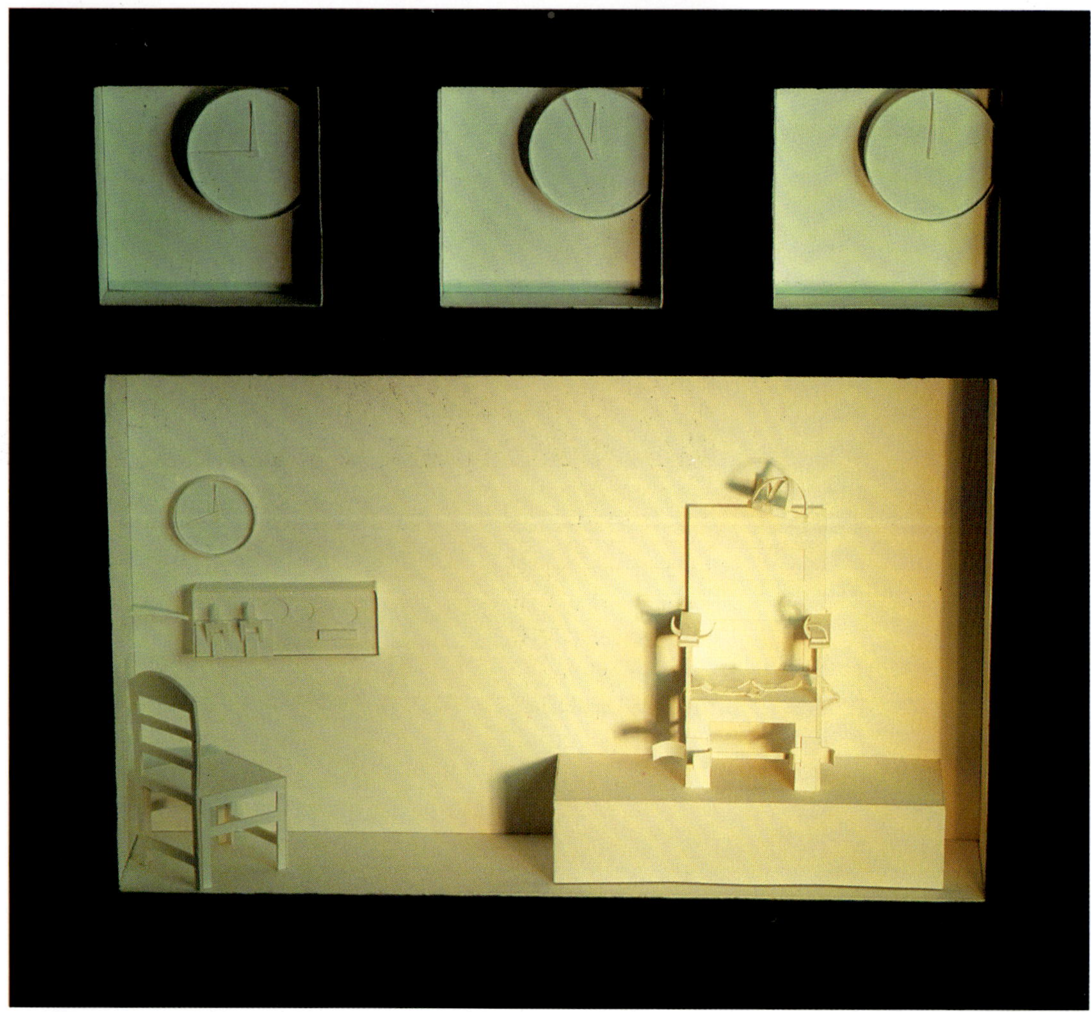

Innocent

3-D Illustrator: Kinley W. Borden
Art Director: Kinley W. Borden
Category: Unpublished

Dragon

3-D Illustrator: Mary Jo Pauly
Photographer: Don Bruno
Client: Lychnobite Design
Category: Unpublished

The Fish

3-D Illustrator: Dennis Valera
Photographer: Dennis Valera
Category: Unpublished

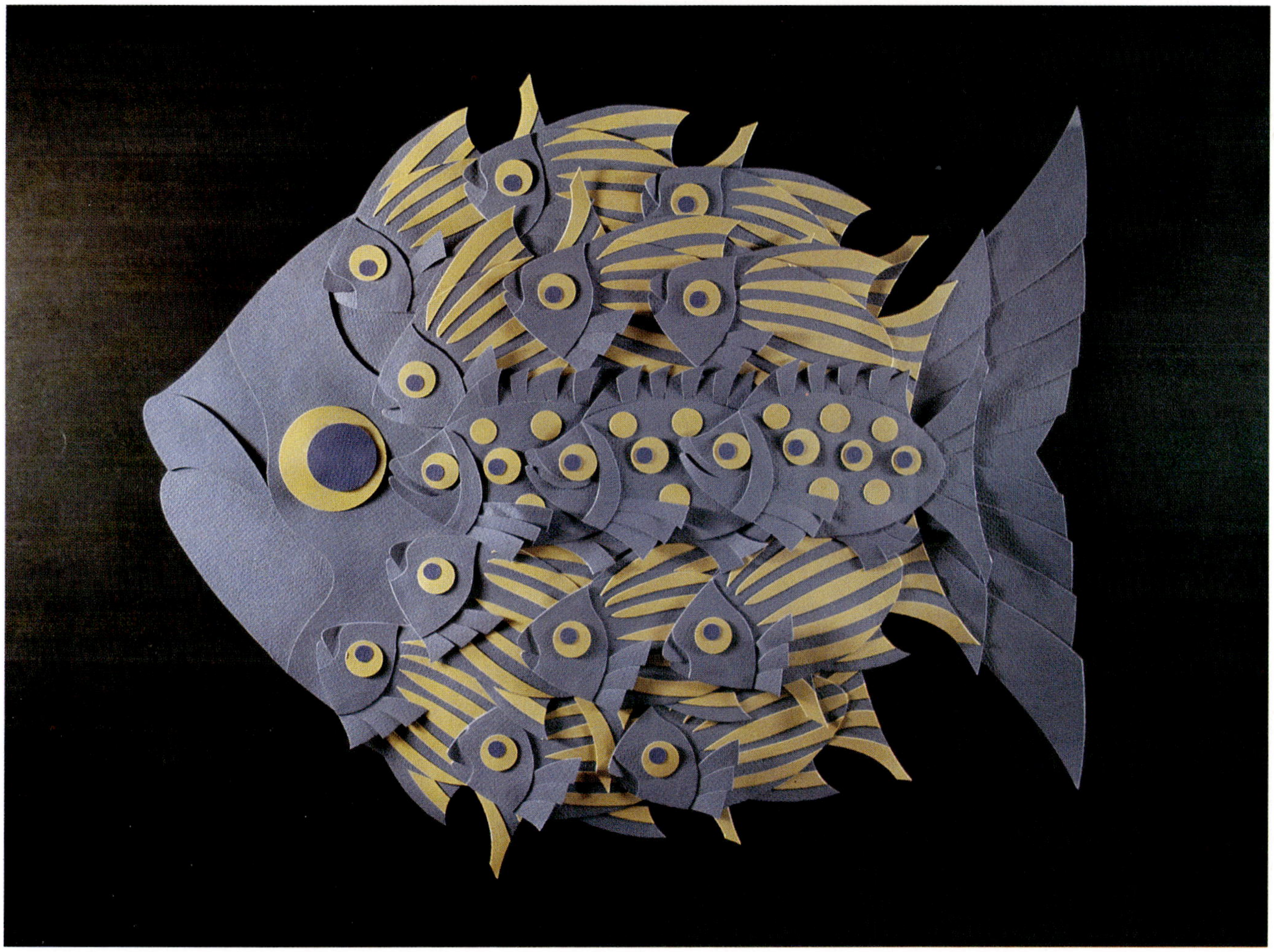

Annually, the advertising print industry is confronted with discovering innovative marketing strategies to augment revenue. Advertising agencies are increasingly relying on 3-D Pop-Ups to achieve this objective. Die-cut pop-ups, double pop-ups and multiple shape designs are employed to reinforce the advertising message. Dimensional inserts generate greater reader involvement, improve overall response and ultimately, increase revenue. The proliferation of pop-ups demonstrates the industry's recognition of this medium as an important adjunct of dimensional illustration.

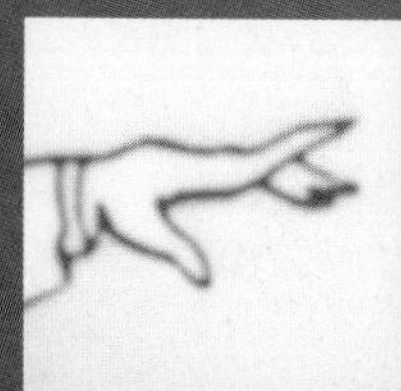

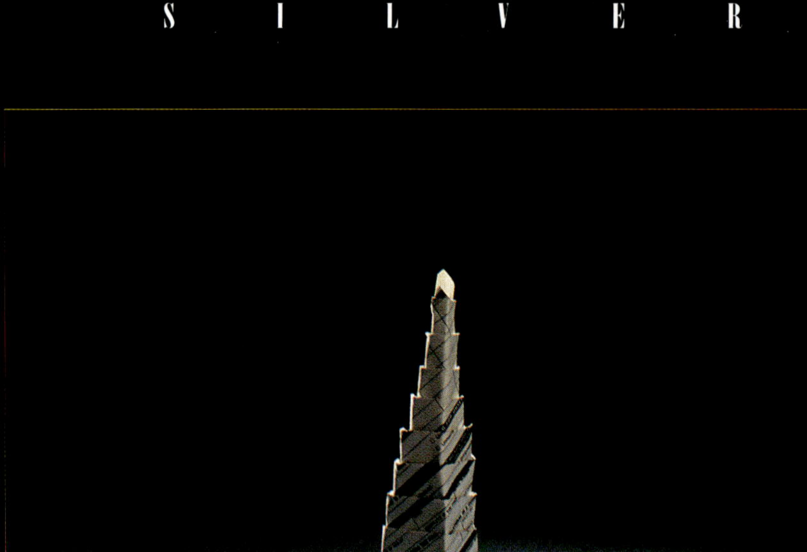

Origami

Animator: Roland Houle
Art Director: Bill Jarcho
Director: Judy Rubin
Studio: Olive Jar Animation
Agency: Ketchum Advertising
Client: Pittsburgh National Bank
Category: TV Commercial

Victorian House

3-D Illustrator: Hal Lōse
Art Director: Hal Lōse
Photographer: Howard Gale
Agency: Al Paul Lefton
Client: Rohm & Haas
Category: Advertising Business Direct Mail Brochure

Swissôtel

3-D Illustrator: Intervisual Communications
Art Director: Juergen Dahlen
Photographer: John Manno
Agency: Graf Bertel Dominique
Client: Swissôtel
Category: Advertising Business Direct Mail Brochure

Summit

3-D Illustrator: Lizanne Elaine Webb
Art Director: Lizanne Elaine Webb
Agency: Studio 22
Client: Lizanne Elaine Webb
Category: Self Promotion Card

Cityscape With Giant Cockroach

3-D Illustrator: Joan Kritchman/Knuteson
Art Director: Keith Wattling
Photographer: Joe Beauchamp
Agency: Bader Rutter & Associates
Client: Dow Elanco
Category: Advertising Business Direct Mail Brochure

Harlow's

3-D Illustrator: William R. Ives
Art Director: William R. Ives
Photographer: Bob Grubb & Son, Inc.
Agency: Ives Design
Category: Greeting Card

Babe's

3-D Illustrator: William R. Ives
Art Director: William R. Ives
Photographer: Bob Grubb & Sons, Inc.
Agency: Ives Design
Category: Greeting Card

Halloween Greetings

3-D Illustrator: John Simonetti
Art Director: John Simonetti
Photographer: Arlene Brown
Agency: Dimensional Design Company
Category: Greeting Card Campaign

Victorian Christmas Advent Calendar

3-D Illustrator: Susan Tyrrell
Art Director: Susan Tyrrell
Photographer: Jan Bindas Studio
Agency: Ruby Shoes Studio
Client: Museum of Fine Arts Boston
Publisher: Museum of Fine Arts Boston
Category: Calendar

Historically, fabric and stitchery have been culturally indispensable. Although underutilized in the past as an illustrative medium, fabric has been instrumental in the creation of textural illustrations which evoke a positive viewer reaction. Creative directors are recognizing the visual appeal of fabric as an alternative illustrative medium. Illustrations are created in the form of collage, soft sculpture or a combination of stitchery and material. The blending of patterns, tones and textures has led to the acceptance of fabric as a viable 3-D medium.

FRANK · GUMPERT · PRINTING

"STUDY IN APPLES" · ONE IN A SERIES BY JERRY PAVEY

Study In Apples

3-D Illustrator: Jerry Pavey
Art Director: Jerry Pavey
Photographer: Photo Response Studio
Agency: Jerry Pavey Design & Illustration
Publisher: Frank Gumpert Printing Company
Client: Frank Gumpert Printing Company/Jerry Pavey
Category: Self Promotion Poster

Fruit Stand

3-D Illustrator: Margaret Cusack
Art Director: Lori Weber
Photographer: Ron Breland
Publisher: Consumer Digest Magazine
Client: Consumer Digest Magazine
Category: Miscellaneous

Bed And Breakfast Spread

3-D Illustrator: Anne Cook
Art Director: J. Porter
Photographer: Will Mosgrove
Agency: Yankee Magazine
Publisher: Yankee Publishing
Client: Yankee Magazine
Category: Business Magazine Spread

Dow Corning Makes A World Of Difference

3-D Illustrator: Margaret Cusack
Art Director: Frank Cusack
Photographer: Skip Caplan
Agency: HDM Advertising
Client: Dow Corning
Category: Advertising Consumer Magazine Full Page

Diversity And Democracy

3-D Illustrator: Jerry Pavey
Art Director: Andrew Bornstein
Photographer: Photo Response Studio
Agency: Jerry Pavey Design & Illustration
Publisher: American Federation of Teachers/AFL-CIO
Client: American Educator Magazine
Category: Editorial Consumer Magazine Full Page

DIVERSITY AND DEMOCRACY

Multicultural Education in America

BY DIANE RAVITCH

Particularism: n. 1. Exclusive adherence to or interest in one's own group, party, sect, or nation. 2. A policy of allowing each state in a nation or federation to act independently.

THE HISTORY of American public education contains numerous examples of racial, religious, and ethnic conflict. This is not surprising, since the schools tend to be the most sensitive cultural barometers in society. The curriculum of the schools is often seen by parents, policy makers, and interest groups as a means to shape the minds and values of the next generation. As long as there has been public education in this country, the schools have provided an arena for social conflict in which groups clash over whose values are taught in the schools.

During the nineteenth century, Catholics fought to remove the Protestant influence on textbooks and curricula. Battles over school prayer and over the presence of religious activities in school still divide communities nearly thirty years after the Supreme Court forbade prayer in the schools. The advance of secularism has prompted fundamentalist Christians to campaign against textbooks and library books that offend their religious views and for science courses that teach creationism on an equal footing with evolution. For the past four decades, the movement to eliminate racial segregation and its lingering effects from the schools has changed the nature of American schools and American society.

Although educators and policy makers must strive to keep the schools free from partisan struggles, the schools inevitably are drawn into controversies that reflect the differences in values among people in a diverse society. Sometimes these controversies have been ultimately beneficial to the schools, for example, by ending racial segregation, by removing biased materials from textbooks, or by creating programs to encourage more girls to study mathematics and science.

But not all controversies have happy outcomes; not all stories have happy endings. Textbooks suffer, as does instruction, when publishers remove literary selections with myths or fables or themes that offend someone, somewhere. Science programs are weakened when teachers are afraid to teach about AIDS or sex education or evolution because some parents object. History instruction is distorted when interest groups exert political pressure on teachers, textbook publishers, and school board members to have the past taught their way.

Diane Ravitch is adjunct professor of history and education at Teachers College, Columbia University; author of "Troubled Crusade: American Education 1945-1980"; *and co-writer of the* California History-Social Science Framework.

16 AMERICAN EDUCATOR — SPRING 1990

Kwikset Nighttime Ad

3-D Illustrator: Margaret Cusack
Art Director: Ron Ho
Photographer: Skip Caplan
Agency: Evans/LA
Client: Kwikset Locks
Category: Advertising Consumer Magazine Full Page

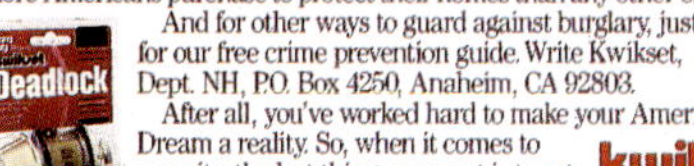

Old-Fashioned Sampler

3-D Illustrator: Margaret Cusack
Art Director: Ralph Pucci
Photographer: Ron Breland
Agency: Solin Associates
Client: Aunt Millie's Spaghetti
Category: Advertising Consumer Magazine Full Page

Loan Sweet Loan

3-D Illustrator: Margaret Cusack
Art Director: Bill Santry
Agency: Earle Palmer Brown
Client: Freddi Mac
Category: Advertising Direct Mail Consumer

Dowper Magazine Spread

3-D Illustrator: Vicky Elsom
Art Director: Lynn Ridley
Photographer: Ray Boudreau
Agency: Kelley Advertising, Inc./Canada
Publisher: Canadian Cleaner & Launderer
Client: Dow Chemical Canada, Inc.
Category: Advertising Business Magazine Spread

DOWPER* SOLVENT

The All-Season Solution To Clean Clothes

Season after season, year after year, the performance of DOWPER solvent has made it the perchloroethylene chosen by more drycleaners than any other. When you use DOWPER solvent, you know you've got what it takes to keep customers happy, because DOWPER solvent brings out the clean, fresh best in good clothes.

DOWPER solvent can: • reduce lint build-up and transfer • prevent fabric discolouration • minimize wrinkling and shrinkage, and is • easy to use and • recyclable.

The All-Reason Solution To Safety And The Environment

Dow Chemical Canada and our authorized distributors are fully committed to providing you with the best product and service possible.

As the world's largest supplier of perchloroethylene, we share with you the responsibility of encouraging the safe handling and disposal of DOWPER solvent. Providing the necessary information, education, and motivation is of benefit to us all. Please contact your DOWPER solvent distributor for more information.

Insist On DOWPER Solvent. The All-Season, All-Reason Solution.

DOW

*Trademark of The Dow Chemical Company

SSMC Annual Report

3-D Illustrator: Margaret Cusack
Art Director: Yoav Polatnik
Photographer: Ron Breland
Agency: Corporate Annual Reports
Client: SSMC
Category: Complete Annual Report

Dowper Solvent Calendar

3-D Illustrator: Vicky Elsom
Art Director: Lynn Ridley
Photographer: Ray Boudreau
Agency: Kelley Advertising, Inc./Canada
Client: Dow Chemical Canada, Inc.
Category: Complete Calendar

Dowper Solvent Poster

3-D Illustrator: Vicky Elsom
Art Director: Lynn Ridley
Photographer: Ray Boudreau
Agency: Kelley Advertising, Inc./Canada
Client: Dow Chemical Canada, Inc.
Category: Self Promotion Poster

Dowper Solvent Post Cards

3-D Illustrator: Vicky Elsom
Art Director: Lynn Ridley
Photographer: Ray Boudreau
Agency: Kelley Advertising, Inc./Canada
Client: Dow Chemical Canada, Inc.
Category: Advertising Business Direct Mail

Healthy Pregnancy Posters

3-D Illustrator: Chris Bobin
Art Director: Russell Brightwell
Photographer: Jack Reznicki
Agency: Botto, Roessner, Horne & Messinger
Client: Armour Pharmaceutical Company
Category: Advertising Business Direct Mail Poster

Legs And Feathers

3-D Illustrator: Anne Cook
Art Director: Barry Shapiro
Photographer: Will Mosgrove
Agency: FCB/LA
Client: Emjoi
Category: Miscellaneous

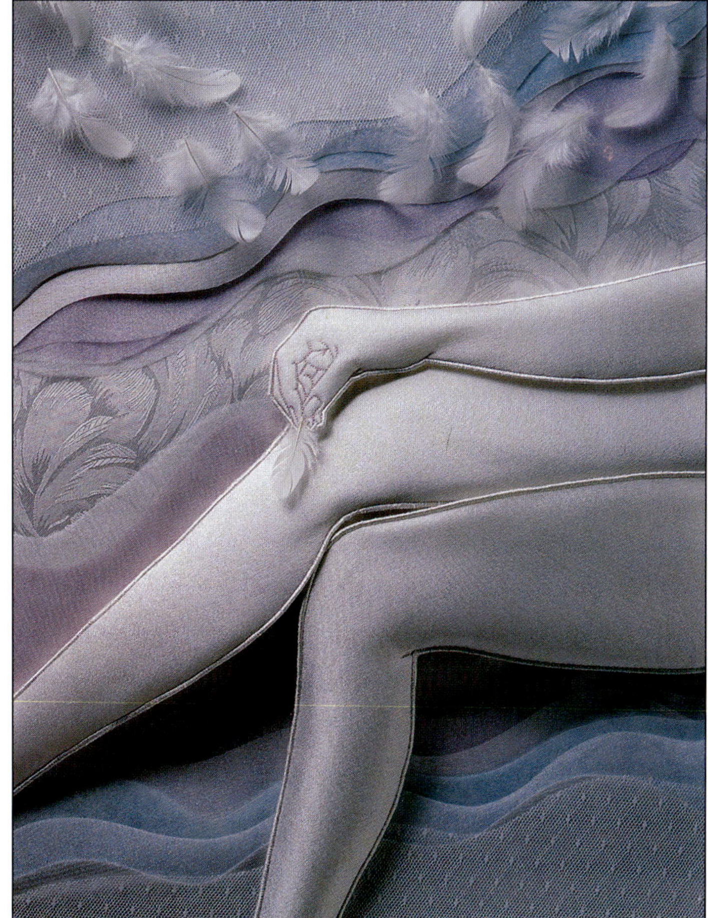

Silk Cut Chain Saw

3-D Illustrator: Nancy Fouts
Art Director: Gerry Hollens
Photographer: Graham Ford
Agency: Saatchi & Saatchi
Client: Gallaher
Category: Advertising Consumer Magazine

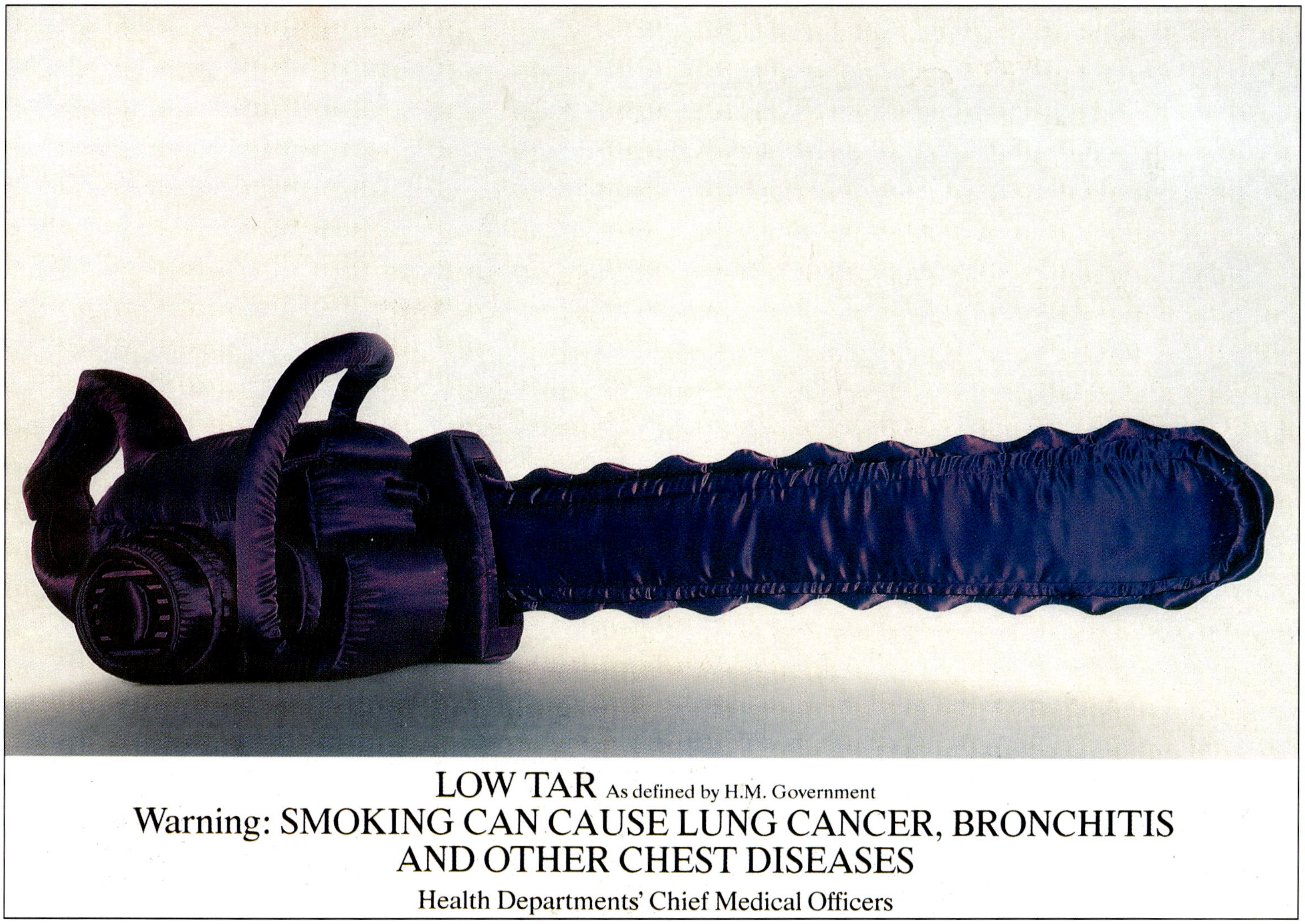

LOW TAR As defined by H.M. Government
Warning: SMOKING CAN CAUSE LUNG CANCER, BRONCHITIS AND OTHER CHEST DISEASES
Health Departments' Chief Medical Officers

Santa

3-D Illustrator: Margaret Cusack
Art Director: Rubin Pfeffer
Photographer: Ron Breland
Publisher: Greene Cross/H.B.J.
Client: Greene Cross/H.B.J.
Category: Greeting Card

Lion And Lamb

3-D Illustrator: Jerry Pavey
Art Director: Jerry Pavey
Photographer: Photo Response Studio
Agency: Jerry Pavey Design & Illustration
Publisher: Frank Gumpert Printing Company
Client: Frank Gumpert Printing Company
Category: Greeting Card

It's All In Your Head

3-D Illustrator: Bonnie J. Lallky
Art Director: Lynn Occhiuzzo
Photographer: Anne Ryan
Publisher: News/Sun-Sentinel
Category: Newspaper Full Page

Home For Christmas

3-D Illustrator: Margaret Cusack
Art Director: Robin Bray/Rubin Pfeffer
Agency: Time Life Music/H.B.J.
Publisher: Time Life Music/H.B.J.
Client: Time Life Music/H.B.J.
Category: Record Cover

Equity Billboard

3-D Illustrator: Anne Cook
Art Director: Tony Smith
Photographer: Will Mosgrove
Agency: McCann Erikson/SF
Client: Wells Fargo Bank
Category: Billboard

Nike Air

3-D Illustrator: Anne Cook
Art Director: Anne Cook
Photographer: Will Mosgrove
Client: Anne Cook
Category: Self Promotion Post Card

Wisconsin Blue Jay

3-D Illustrators: James & Shirley Wagner
Art Director: James Wagner
Photographer: Ferderbar Studios
Agency: Art Factory
Client: Art Factory
Category: Calendar Full Page

The Happy Hands

3-D Illustrator: Ellen Rixford
Art Director: Greg Cordell
Photographer: Ellen Rixford
Agency: Greg & Greg, Creative
Client: Pat Chem
Category: Advertising Illustration

4TH ANNUAL CALL FOR ENTRIES INFORMATION

The 4th Annual Dimensional Illustrators Awards Show featuring the Gold, Silver and Merit award winners will be held the week of November 29th, 1992 at the Art Directors Club of New York. Gold and Silver award winners will also be exhibited at the Fouts and Fowler Gallery, London, England in the spring of 1992. As we enter our fourth year of competition, we are continuing our efforts to recognize and honor the contemporary 3-Dimensional Illustrators, art directors and visual creatives of the 90's. This international competition is committed to showcasing the best in 3-Dimensional Illustration worldwide.

Dimensional Illustrators, Inc. invites you to participate in this most prestigious exhibition by entering the 4th Annual Dimensional Illustrators Awards Show. Join the world's most talented professionals in their efforts to demonstrate the versatility and technical excellence of the contemporary 3-Dimensional Illustration industry.

Call For Entries Deadline: May 31, 1992

For information contact:
Nick Greco/Awards Show Coordinator.

Dimensional Illustrators, Inc.
362 Second Street Pike/Suite 112
Southampton, Pennsylvania 18966

Telephone: (215) 953-1415
Fax: (215) 953-1697

Kathleen Ziegler and Nick Greco, founders of Dimensional Illustrators, Inc., specialize in creating 3-Dimensional Illustrations for the visual communications industry. An accomplished illustrator and lecturer, Kathleen creates 3-Dimensional models and props for the advertising, pharmaceutical and publishing industries. Models are produced in plastic, acrylic, clay, wood, foam and paper. Special effects photography is used to create ingenious 3-Dimensional images.

Principal partner Nick Greco, coordinates the marketing decisions which have established Dimensional Illustrators, Inc., as one of the industry's leading 3-Dimensional studios. Nick concentrates his efforts on the business of 3-Dimensional Illustration, including pricing, rights and resale guidelines and coordinates special projects.

Their work has appeared in the nation's leading publications including Discover, RN, Health, Nursing, Learning, Medical Economics, Emergency Medicine, Drug Therapy, Diagnosis and Geriatrics. The studio has received awards from the Association of Medical Illustrators Show, Desi Awards Show, RX Club and the Philadelphia Art Directors Club. In addition, they recently received the AGFA Achievement in Design Award.

Dimensional Illustrators, Inc. produces the 3-Dimensional Illustrators Awards Show and Exhibition which recognizes the highly talented visual creatives responsible for the growth of the 3-Dimensional industry. The success of this show has resulted in the publication of ***3-Dimensional Illustrators Awards Annual II/The Best In 3-D Advertising And Publishing Worldwide.***

Mediums Include:

3-Dimensional Animation
3-Dimensional Photography
3-D Biography
3-D Medical
Assemblage
Cake & Icing Sculpture
Ceramic Tile
Clay Sculpture
Copper Sculpture
Costumes
Cut Paper Assemblage
Dyed Leather Assemblage
Effects
Fabric Collage
Foam Rubber
Foam Sculpture
Food Sculpture
Found Objects Collage
Gingerbread
Handmade Paper Collage
Latex Rubber
Life Masks
Metal Sculpture
Miniature Sets
Mixed Media Assemblage
Mixed Media Collage
Mixed Media
Modelmaking
Natura Assemblages
Painted Wood
Paper Collage
Paper Engineering
Paper Mâché
Paper Pop-Ups
Paper Sculpture
Plaster
Plastic Sculpture
Polyurethane Foams
Puppets
Samplers
Sand Sculpture
Soft Sculpture
Wood Carving
Wood Sculpture

The international directory of 3-Dimensional Illustrators contains the Gold, Silver and Merit award winners of the 2nd Annual Dimensional Illustrators Awards Show. This complete directory presents the most talented 3-Dimensional Illustrators from the United States, Canada and Europe. All Dimensional Illustrators are listed by 3-Dimensional medium of specialization. In addition, illustrators are listed alphabetically.

3-DIMENSIONAL ANIMATION

Alpert, Olive
Olive Alpert/Design
9511 Shore Road/Apt. 111
Brooklyn, NY 11209
718-833-3092

Berman, Jim
Olive Jar Animation
44 White Place
Brookline, MA 02146
617-566-6699

Burns, Sean
Olive Jar Animation
44 White Place
Brookline, MA 02146
617-566-6699

Daley, Carolyn
4665 Refugee Road/Apt.3H
Columbus, OH 43232
614-759-0209

Einsel, Walter
26 South Morningside Drive
Westport, CT 06880
203-226-0709

Frizzell, Mark
P.O. Box 3176
Woburn, MA 01888
617-933-0805

Grimmett, Douglass
1013 Carmel Church Road
Chapel Hill, NC 27514
919-967-6841

Lemmon, John
John Lemmon Films
1216 Pinecrest Avenue
Charlotte, NC 28205
704-532-1944

Manning, Michael
Olive Jar Animation
44 White Place
Brookline, MA 02146
617-566-6699

Molampy, Scott
Geppetto Soft Sculpture & Display
107 Lexington Avenue/4th FL
Brooklyn, NY 11238
718-398-9792

Rosinski, Mike
John Lemmon Films
1216 Pinecrest Avenue
Charlotte, NC 28205
704-532-1944

Saint John, Bob
320 South Street
Portsmouth, NH 03801
603-436-1567

Vinton, Will
Will Vinton Productions
1400 NW 22nd Avenue
Portland, OR 97210
503-225-1130

3-DIMENSIONAL PHOTOGRAPHY

SWITZERLAND

Van der Bie, Esther
Kloesterlistutz #2
Bern, Switzerland 3013
031-428-572

UNITED STATES

Bartlett, Christopher
Bartlett & Associates
2211B Woodbox Lane
Baltimore, MD 21209
301-484-1906

Bono, Mary M.
288 Graham Avenue
Brooklyn, NY 11211
718-387-3774

Carlton, Chuck
Axiom, Inc.
120 South Brook Street
Louisville, KY 40202
502-584-7666

Christensen, Gayle
1026 Maywood Lane
Martinez, CA 94553
415-943-8161

Emmott, Bob
Emmott Photography, Inc.
700 South 10th Street
Philadelphia, PA 19147
215-925-2773

Frick, Thomas
227 Doris Avenue
Baltimore, MD 21225
301-789-3045

Grimmett, Douglass
1013 Carmel Church Road
Chapel Hill, NC 27514
919-967-6841

Hart, Cynthia
Cynthia Hart Designer
902 Broadway/Penthouse
New York, NY 10010
212-475-4660

Klumpp, Susan
989 Vincent Ct.
Westerville, OH 43081
614-891-7593

Koudis, Nick
Nick Koudis Studio
40 East 23rd Street
New York, NY 10010
212-475-2802
(Photographic Special Effects)

Molampy, Scott
Geppetto Soft Sculpture & Display
107 Lexington Avenue/4th FL
Brooklyn, NY 11238
718-398-9792

Murakami, Tak
1535 W Juneway Terrace
Chicago, IL 60626
312-764-7845

Nazz, James
42 Steyvesant Street
New York, NY 10003
212-228-9713

Paperny, Vladimir
Vladimir Paperny & Associates
1114 12th Street, #101
Santa Monica, CA 90403
213-393-7564

Rixford, Ellen
Ellen Rixford Studio
308 West 97th Street/#71
New York, NY 10025
212-865-5686

Saint John, Bob
320 South Street
Portsmouth, NH 03801
603-436-1567

Saksa, Cathy
Saksa Art + Design
41 Union Square West/Suite 1001
New York, NY 10003
212-255-5539

Seman, Ron
The Object Works
12 Eighth Street
Pittsburgh, PA 15222
412-261-3513

Sturm, Linda K.
3 Evergreen Lane
Chappaqua, NY 10514
914-238-8318

Webb, Lizanne Elaine
Studio 22
PO Box 432
Webster, NY 14580
716-265-4542

Ziegler, Kathleen
Dimensional Illustrators, Inc.
362 2nd Street Pike/Suite 112
Southampton, PA 18966
215-953-1415/Fax 215-953-1697

3-D MEDICAL

Yurkiw, Mark
Mark Yurkiw, Ltd.
568 Broadway/Suite 605
New York, NY 10012
212-226-6338

Ziegler, Kathleen
Dimensional Illustrators, Inc
362 2nd Street Pike/Suite 112
Southampton, PA 18966
215-953-1415 /Fax 215-953-1697

3-D BIOGRAPHY

Browne, Rob
541 Winterberry Way
San Jose, CA 95129
408-255-8843

ASSEMBLAGE

Hall, Joan
155 Bank Street/H954
New York, NY 10014
212-243-6059

CAKE & ICING SCULPTURE

Littman, Rosemary
Rosemary's Cakes
299 Rutland Avenue
Teaneck, NJ 07666
201-833-2417

CERAMIC TILE

Pavey, Jerry
Jerry Pavey Design & Illustration
507 Orchard Way
Silver Spring, MD 20904
301-384-3377
(Ceramic Tile & Grout Assemblages)

CLAY SCULPTURE

CANADA

Chatwin, Robert
3-D Illustrator
25 Winnett Avenue
Toronto, Ontario Canada M6C 3L2
416-657-8133

ENGLAND

Fowler, Malcolm
Shirt Sleeve Studio
52 Oakley Square
The Old Vicarage
London, England NW1 1NJ
071-388-6491

SCOTLAND

Watson, Douglas
2 Leadervale Road
Edinburgh, Scotland UK EH16 6PA
031-664-2524

UNITED STATES

Alpert, Olive
Olive Alpert/Design
9511 Shore Road/Apt. 111
Brooklyn, NY 11209
718-833-3092

Arroyo, Andrea
Andrea Arroyo Studio
PO Box 1472
New York, NY 10009-8904
212-477-2485

Bartlett, Christopher
Bartlett & Associates
2211B Woodbox Lane
Baltimore, MD 21209
301-484-1906

Berman, Simi
Box 58
Chesterfield, NH 03443
603-256-8477

Blauers, Nancy
50 Walnut Street
Stratford, CT 06497
203-377-6109

Bono, Mary M.
288 Graham Avenue
Brooklyn, NY 11211
718-387-3774

Christensen, Gayle
1026 Maywood Lane
Martinez, CA 94553
415-943-8161

Daley, Carolyn
4665 Refugee Road/Apt 3H
Columbus, OH 43232
614-759-0209

Falls, Mark
The Mark Falls Corporation
605 Lincoln Road/Suite 410
Miami Beach, FL 33319
305-532-7573

Foord, Mimi
Smaller Than Life Productions
1595 Stanford Street
Concord, CA 94519
415-680-0493

Frick, Thomas
227 Doris Avenue
Baltimore, MD 21225
301-789-3045

Frizzell, Mark
P.O. Box 3176
Woburn, MA 01888
617-933-0805

Gay-Kassel, Doreen
24a Chestnut Ct.
Princeton, NJ 08540
609-497-0783

Goodman, Michael L.
1922 Windingridge Drive
Richmond, VA 23233
804-771-9331

Graham, Jack
Graham Illustration
4415 E. Ashurst Drive
Phoenix, AZ 85044
602-759-9353

Grimmett, Douglass
1013 Carmel Church Road
Chapel Hill, NC 27514
919-967-6841

Hazlerig, Mark L.
F/X Illustration
3619 Washburn Street
Columbus, OH 43213
614-239-9290

Jeffers, Kathy
151 West 19th Street/3rd FL
New York, NY 10011
212-255-5196

Klumpp, Susan
989 Vincent Ct.
Westerville, OH 43081
614-891-7593

Kritchman/Knuteson, Joan
Advertising Art Studios, Inc.
710 North Plankinton
Milwaukee, WI 53203
414-276-6306

Lallky-Seibert, Bonnie J.
161 N.E. 38th Street, #19-B
Ft. Lauderdale, FL 33334
305-564-3259

Lemmon, John
John Lemmon Films
1216 Pinecrest Avenue
Charlotte, NC 28205
704-532-1944

McNeel, Richard
530 Valley Road/#2G
Upper Montclair, NJ 07043
201-509-2255

Murakami, Tak
1535 W. Juneway Terrace
Chicago, IL 60626
312-764-7845

Nachreiner, Tom
Art Factory
925 Elm Grove Road
Elm Grove, WI 53122
414-785-1940

Rixford, Ellen
Ellen Rixford Studio
308 West 97th Street/#71
New York, NY 10025
212-865-5686

Rosinski, Mike
John Lemmon Films
1216 Pinecrest Avenue
Charlotte, NC 28205
704-532-1944

Saint John, Bob
320 South Street
Portsmouth, NH 03801
603-436-1567

Sanders, James
Get Up And Gourmet. Inc.
2066 Lyric Avenue
Los Angeles, CA 90039
213-669-1879

Selby, Bob
Providence Journal
75 Fountain Street
Providence, RI 02902
401-277-7257

Seman, Ron
The Object Works
12 Eighth Street
Pittsburgh, PA 15222
412-261-3513

Sievers, Lee & Mary
Sievers' Studio
5516 Queen Avenue South
Minneapolis, MN 55410
612-929-1726

Sturm, Linda K.
3 Evergreen Lane
Chappaqua, NY 10514
914-238-8318

Suyeoka, George
699 Sheridan Road
Evanston, IL 60202
708-475-1090

Swenarton, Gordon
Falcone & Associates
13 Watchung Avenue
Chatham, NJ 07928
201-635-2900

Vinton, Will
Will Vinton Productions
1400 NW 22nd Avenue
Portland, OR 97210
503-225-1130

Workman, Jef
Bird In The Hand Studio
310 Carmel Avenue
Pacific Grove, CA 93950
408-372-9010

Ziegler, Kathleen
Dimensional Illustrators, Inc.
362 2nd Street Pike/Suite 112
Southampton, PA 18966
215-953-1415/Fax 215-953-1697

COPPER SCULPTURE

Miller, Bill
Bill Miller/Illustration
1355 N. Sandburg Terrace
Suite 2002 D
Chicago, IL 60610
312-787-4093

COSTUMES

Bobin, Chris
5 East 17th Street/6th FL
New York, NY 10003
212-691-2821/212-475-7268

CUT PAPER ASSEMBLAGE

Hahn, Eileen
8 Hillwood Road
East Brunswick, NJ 08816
908-390-4188

DYED LEATHER ASSEMBLAGE

Pavey, Jerry
Jerry Pavey Design & Illustration
507 Orchard Way
Silver Spring, MD 20904
301-384-3377
(Dyed Leather Assemblages with Nails, Brads & Tacks)

EFFECTS

Yurkiw, Mark
Mark Yurkiw Ltd.
568 Broadway/Suite #605
New York, NY 10012
212-226-6338

FABRIC COLLAGE

CANADA

Elsom, Vicky
Vicky Elsom Design
95 Lawton Blvd/607
Toronto, Ontario/Canada M4V 128
416-489-6453

ENGLAND

Fouts, Nancy
Shirt Sleeve Studio
52 Oakley Square
The Old Vicarage
London, England NW1 1NJ
071-388-6491

UNITED STATES

Alpert, Olive
Olive Alpert/Design
9511 Shore Road/Apt.111
Brooklyn, NY 11209
718-833-3092

Bobin, Chris
5 East 17th Street/6th FL
New York, NY 10003
212-691-2821/212-475-7268

Christensen, Gayle
1026 Maywood Lane
Martinez, CA 94553
415-943-8161

Cook, Anne
Anne Cook Textile Art & Illus.
96 Rollingwood Drive
San Rafael, CA 94901
415-454-5799

FABRIC COLLAGE
(Continued)

UNITED STATES
Cusack, Margaret
124 Hoyt Street
Brooklyn, NY 11217-2215
718-237-0145

Einsel, Walter
26 S. Morningside Drive
Westport, CT 06880
203-226-0709

Finewood, Bill
Art Works, Inc.
605 Main Street
East Rochester, NY 14445
716-377-3126

Hart, Cynthia
Cynthia Hart Designer
902 Broadway/Penthouse
New York, NY 10010
212-475-4660

Klumpp, Susan
989 Vincent Ct.
Westerville, OH 43081
614-891-7593

Kritchman/Knuteson, Joan
Advertising Art Studios, Inc.
710 North Plankinton
Milwaukee, WI 53203
414-276-6306

Lallky-Seibert, Bonnie J.
161 N.E. 38th Street, #19-B
Ft.Lauderdale, FL 33334
305-564-3259

Pavey, Jerry
Jerry Pavey Design & Illustration
507 Orchard Way
Silver Spring, MD 20904
301-384-3377

Rixford, Ellen
Ellen Rixford Studio
308 West 97th Street/#71
New York, NY 10025
212-865-5686

Saint John, Bob
320 South Street
Portsmouth, NH 03801
603-436-1567

Saksa, Cathy
Saksa Art + Design
41 Union Square West/Suite 1001
New York, NY 10003
212-255-5539

Wagner, James & Shirley
Art Factory
925 Elm Grove Road
Elm Grove, WI 53122
414-785-1940

FOAM RUBBER
Hazlerig, Mark L.
F/X Illustration
3619 Washburn Street
Columbus, OH 43213
614-239-9290

FOAM SCULPTURE
Bobin, Chris
5 East 17th Street/6th FL
New York, NY 10003
212-691-2821/212-475-7268

Field, Bob
336 Washington Street
Brookline, MA 02146
617-232-2230

Molampy, Scott
Geppetto Soft Sculpture & Display
107 Lexington Avenue/4th FL
Brooklyn, NY 11238
718-398-9792

Ziegler, Kathleen
Dimensional Illustrators, Inc
362 2nd Street Pike/Suite 112
Southampton, PA 18966
215-953-1415/Fax 215-953-1697

FOOD SCULPTURE
Alpert, Olive
Olive Alpert/Design
9511 Shore Road/Apt.111
Brooklyn, NY 11209
718-833-3092
(Gingerbread)

Littman, Rosemary
Rosemary's Cakes
299 Rutland Avenue
Teaneck, NJ 07666
201-833-2417
(Cake & Icing)

Yurkiw, Mark
Mark Yurkiw Ltd.
568 Broadway/Suite 605
New York, NY 10012
212-226-6338

FOUND OBJECTS COLLAGE
ENGLAND
Fouts, Nancy
Shirt Sleeve Studio
52 Oakley Square
The Old Vicarage
London, England NW1 1NJ
071-388-6491

UNITED STATES
Einsel, Walter
26 South Morningside Drive
Westport, CT 06880
203-226-0709

GINGERBREAD
Alpert, Olive
Olive Alpert/Design
9511 Shore Road/Apt.111
Brooklyn, NY 11209
718-833-3092

HANDMADE PAPER COLLAGE
Corfield, Marie
48 Sylvan Place
Nutley, NJ 07110
201-667-8071

LATEX RUBBER
Daley, Carolyn
4665 Refugee Road/Apt.3H
Columbus, OH 43232
614-759-0209

Hazlerig, Mark L.
F/X Illustration
3619 Washburn Street
Columbus, OH 43213
614-239-9290

Klumpp, Susan
989 Vincent Ct.
Westerville, OH 43081
614-891-7593

LIFE MASKS
Klumpp, Susan
989 Vincent Ct.
Westerville, OH 43081
614-891-7593

METAL SCULPTURE
CANADA
Fleming, Joe
Joe Fleming Illustration
487 Mortimer Avenue
Toronto, Canada M4J2G6
416-466-0630

UNITED STATES
Hazlerig, Mark L.
F/X Illustration
3619 Washburn Street
Columbus, OH 43213
614-239-9290

Murakami, Tak
1535 W. Juneway Terrace
Chicago, IL 60626
312-764-7845

Pavey, Jerry
Jerry Pavey Design & Illustration
507 Orchard Way
Silver Spring, MD 20904
301-384-3377
(Metal Sculpture with Nuts,
Bolts & Screws)

Rasmussen, Bonnie
A.Art/B.Rasmussen, Ltd.
8828 Pendleton
St. Louis, MO 63144
314-962-1842/Fax 314-962-4816

Seman, Ron
The Object Works
12 Eighth Street
Pittsburgh, PA 15222
412-261-3513

MINIATURE SETS
Nazz, James
42 Steyvesant Street
New York, NY 10003
212-228-9713

MIXED MEDIA ASSEMBLAGE
Rasmussen, Bonnie
A.Art/B.Rasmussen, Ltd.
8828 Pendleton
St. Louis, MO 63144
314-962-1842/Fax 314-962-4816

MIXED MEDIA COLLAGE
Maraschiello, Frank
520 2nd Avenue
New York, NY 10016
212-889-6012

MIXED MEDIA
ENGLAND
Fowler, Malcolm
Shirt Sleeve Studio
52 Oakley Square
The Old Vicarage
London, England NW1 1NJ
071-388-6491

GERMANY
Kiel, Achim
Pencil Corporate Art
Kulturzentrum Rundbogen
Heinrich-Buessing-Hof D-3300
Braunschweig, Lower Saxony/Germany
0531-72964

SCOTLAND
Watson, Douglas
2 Leadervale Road
Edinburgh, Scotland UK EH16 6PA
031-664-2524

SWITZERLAND
Gasser, Philip
Kraftstr, 11
Basel, Switzerland 4056
061-322-1412

Van der Bie, Esther
Kloesterlistutz #2
Bern, Switzerland 3013
031-428-572

UNITED STATES

Alpert, Olive
Olive Alpert/Design
9511 Shore Road/Apt.111
Brooklyn, NY 11209
718-833-3092

Arroyo, Andrea
Andrea Arroyo Studio
PO Box 1472
New York, NY 10009-8904
212-477-2485

Bandle, Johnna
J B Illustration
7726 Noland Rd.
Lenexa, KS 66216
913-962-9595

Bartlett, Christopher
Bartlett & Associates
2211B Woodbox Lane
Baltimore, MD 21209
301-484-1906

Bono, Mary M.
288 Graham Avenue
Brooklyn, NY 11211
718-387-3774

Borden, Kinley W.
1305 Grandview Street
Dunmore, PA 18509
717-253-7901

Botsis, Peter
Botsis Studio
2467 Culver Road
Rochester, NY 14609
716-288-7080

Browne, Rob
541 Winterberry Way
San Jose, CA 95129
408-255-8843

Burnett, Lindy
476 Loridans Drive
Atlanta, GA 30342
404-843-0166

Burns, Sean
Olive Jar Animation
44 White Place
Brookline, MA 02146
617-566-6699

Cable, Jerry
Jerry Cable Design
133 Kuhl Road
Flemington, NJ 08822
908-788-8673/Fax 908-788-8673

Carlton, Chuck
Axiom, Inc.
120 So. Brook Street
Louisville, KY 40202
502-584-7666

Christensen, Gayle
1026 Maywood Lane
Martinez, CA 94553
415-943-8161

Corfield, Marie
48 Sylvan Place
Nutley, NJ 07110
201-667-8071

Daley, Carolyn
4665 Refugee Road/Apt.3H
Columbus, OH 43232
614-759-0209

Einsel, Walter
26 South Morningside Drive
Westport, CT 06880
203-226-0709

Eldridge, Gary
163 South Center Street
Lowell, MI 49331
616-897-6668

Emmott, Bob
Emmott Photography, Inc.
700 South 10th Street
Philadelphia, PA 19147
215-925-2773

Finewood, Bill
Art Works, Inc
605 Main Street
East Rochester, NY 14445
716-377-3126

Frick, Thomas
227 Doris Avenue
Baltimore, MD 21225
301-789-3045

Frizzell, Mark
P.O. Box 3176
Woburn, MA 01888
617-933-0805

Gay-Kassel, Doreen
24a Chestnut Ct.
Princeton, NJ 08540
609-497-0783

Goodman, Michael L.
1922 Windingridge Drive
Richmond, VA 23233
804-771-9331

Grimmett, Douglass
1013 Carmel Church Road
Chapel Hill, NC 27514
919-967-6841

Hall, Joan
155 Bank Street/H954
New York, NY 10014
212-243-6059

Hart, Cynthia
Cynthia Hart Designer
902 Broadway Penthouse
New York, NY 10010
212-475-4660

Hazlerig, Mark L.
F/X Illustration
3619 Washburn Street
Columbus, OH 43213
614-239-9290

Hoffman, Joanne
Hoffman Studios
826 Kater Street
Philadelphia, PA 19147
215-928-9365

Jeffers, Kathy
151 West 19th Street/3rdFL
New York, NY 10011
212-255-5196

Kagan-Batelman, Jill
47-16 39th Avenue
Sunnyside, NY 11104
718-392-3483

Klumpp, Susan
989 Vincent Ct.
Westerville, OH 43081
614-891-7593

Koudis, Nick
Nick Koudis Studio
40 East 23rd Street
New York, NY 10010
212-475-2802

Kritchman/Knuteson, Joan
Advertising Art Studios, Inc.
710 North Plankinton
Milwaukee, WI 53203
414-276-6306

LaMantia, Joe
LaMantia Studio
820 West Howe Street
Bloomington, IN 47403
812-332-2667

Lang, Cecily
250 E Royal Palm Road
Boca Raton, FL 33432
407-392-5860

Manning, Michael
Olive Jar Animation
44 White Place
Brookline, MA 02146
617-566-6699

Maraschiello, Frank
Frank Maraschiello Collage
520 2nd Avenue
New York, NY 10016
212-889-6012

Mikec, Larry
Art Factory
925 Elm Grove Road
Elm Grove, WI 53122
414-785-1940

Murakami, Tak
1535 W. Juneway Terrace
Chicago, IL 60626
312-764-7845

Nazz, James
42 Steyvesant Street
New York, NY 10003
212-228-9713

Otnes, Fred
26 Chalburn Road
West Redding, CT 06896
203-938-2829

Paperny, Vladimir
Vladimir Paperny & Associates
1114 12th Street/#101
Santa Monica, CA 90403
213-393-7564

Pavey, Jerry
Jerry Pavey Design & Illustration
507 Orchard Way
Silver Spring, MD 20904
301-384-3377

Rasmussen, Bonnie
A.Art/B.Rasmussen, Ltd.
8828 Pendleton
St. Louis, MO 63144
314-962-1842/Fax 314-962-4816

Rixford, Ellen
Ellen Rixford Studio
308 West 97th Street/#71
New York, NY 10025
212-865-5686

Saint John, Bob
320 South Street
Portsmouth, NH 03801
603-436-1567

Saksa, Cathy
Saksa Art + Design
41 Union Square West/Suite 1001
New York, NY 10003
212-255-5539

Sanders, James
Get Up And Gourmet. Inc.
2066 Lyric Avenue
Los Angeles, CA 90039
213-669-1879

Seman, Ron
The Object Works
12 Eighth Street
Pittsburgh, PA 15222
412-261-3513

MIXED MEDIA
(Continued)

UNITED STATES

Shohet, Marti
41 Union Square West/Room 1001
New York, NY 10003
212-627-1299

Sievers, Lee & Mary
Sievers' Studio
5516 Queen Avenue South
Minneapolis, MN 55410
612-929-1726

Spencer, Kimberly
Salon Enterprises
1739 Four Mile Road, NE
Grand Rapids, MI 49505
616-363-4000

Steiner, Joan
Bate Road, Box 292, RD 1
Craryville, NY 12521
518-851-7199

Sturm, Linda K.
3 Evergreen Lane
Chappaqua, NY 10514
914-238-8318

Suyeoka, George
699 Sheridan Road
Evanston, IL 60202
708-475-1090

Swenarton, Gordon
Falcone & Associates
13 Watchung Avenue
Chatham, NJ 07928
201-635-2900

Tarrish, Laura
123 Townsend Street/#215
San Francisco, CA 94107
415-442-1866

Traynor, Elizabeth
Elizabeth Traynor Illustration
Rt. 12, Box 32, Barbee Chapel Rd.
Chapel Hill, NC 27514
919-968-6573

Wagner, James & Shirley
Art Factory
925 Elm Grove Road
Elm Grove, WI 53122
414-785-1940

Workman, Jef
Bird In The Hand Studio
310 Carmel Avenue
Pacific Grove, CA 93950
408-372-9010

Yurkiw, Mark
Mark Yurkiw Ltd.
568 Broadway/Suite 605
New York, NY 10012
212-226-6338

MODELMAKING

ENGLAND

Fowler, Malcolm
Shirt Sleeve Studio
52 Oakley Square
The Old Vicarage
London, England NW1 1NJ
071-388-6491

GERMANY

Kiel, Achim
Pencil Corporate Art
Kulturzentrum Rundbogen
Heinrich-Buessing-Hof D-3300
Braunschweig Lower Saxony/Germany
0531-72964

UNITED STATES

Bono, Mary M.
288 Graham Avenue
Brooklyn, NY 11211
718-387-3774

Carlton, Chuck
Axiom, Inc.
120 So. Brook Street
Louisville, KY 40202
502-584-7666

Daley, Carolyn
4665 Refugee Road/Apt.3H
Columbus, OH 43232
614-759-0209

Einsel, Walter
26 South Morningside Drive
Westport, CT 06880
203-226-0709

Emmott, Bob
Emmott Photography, Inc.
700 South 10th Street
Philadelphia, PA 19147
215-925-2773

Falls, Mark
Mark Falls Corporation
605 Lincoln Road/Suite 410
Miami Beach, FL 33319
305-532-7573

Frizzell, Mark
P.O. Box 3176
Woburn, MA 01888
617-933-0805

Goodman, Michael L.
1922 Windingridge Drive
Richmond, VA 23233
804-771-9331

Grimmett, Douglass
1013 Carmel Church Road
Chapel Hill, NC 27514
919-967-6841

Hazlerig, Mark L.
F/X Illustration
3619 Washburn Street
Columbus, OH 43213
614-239-9290

Klumpp, Susan
989 Vincent Ct.
Westerville, OH 43081
614-891-7593

Koudis, Nick
Nick Koudis Studio
40 East 23rd Street
New York, NY 10010
212-475-2802

Kritchman/Knuteson, Joan
Advertising Art Studios, Inc.
710 North Plankinton
Milwaukee, WI 53203
414-276-6306

Manning, Michael
Olive Jar Animation
44 White Place
Brookline, MA 02146
617-566-6699

Miller, Bill
Bill Miller/Illustration
1355 N Sandburg Terrace
Suite 2002 D
Chicago, IL 60610
312-787-4093

Murakami, Tak
1535 W. Juneway Terrace
Chicago, IL 60626
312-764-7845

Nazz, James
42 Steyvesant Street
New York, NY 10003
212-228-9713

Rixford, Ellen
Ellen Rixford Studio
308 West 97th Street/#71
New York, NY 10025
212-865-5686

Saint John, Bob
320 South Street
Portsmouth, NH 03801
603-436-1567

Sanders, James
Get Up And Gourmet, Inc.
2066 Lyric Avenue
Los Angeles, CA 90039
213-669-1879

Schmeelk, William
Wellington Enterprises
55 Railroad Avenue
Garnerville, NY 10923
914-429-3377

Seman, Ron
The Object Works
12 Eighth Street
Pittsburgh, PA 15222
412-261-3513

Tarrish, Laura
123 Townsend Street/#215
San Francisco, CA 94107
415-442-1866

Webb, Lizanne Elaine
Studio 22
PO Box 432
Webster, NY 14580
716-265-4542

Yurkiw, Mark
Mark Yurkiw Ltd.
568 Broadway/Suite #605
New York, NY 10012
212-226-6338

Ziegler, Kathleen
Dimensional Illustrators, Inc.
362 2nd Street Pike/Suite 112
Southampton, PA 18966
215-953-1415/Fax 215-953-1697

NATURA ASSEMBLAGES

Pavey, Jerry
Jerry Pavey Design & Illustration
507 Orchard Way
Silver Spring, MD 20904
301-384-3377
(Natura Assemblages of Wood, Metal, Wire, Rope, Seeds, Grasses, Moss and Pelts)

PAINTED WOOD

CANADA

Fleming, Joe
Joe Fleming Illustration
487 Mortimer Avenue
Toronto, Canada M4J2G6
416-466-0630

PAPER COLLAGE

UNITED STATES

Alpert, Olive
Olive Alpert/Design
9511 Shore Road/Apt.111
Brooklyn, NY 11209
718-833-3092

Baum, Susan
123 Palisade Street
Dobbs Ferry, NY 10522
914-693-5143

Burnett, Lindy
476 Loridans Drive
Atlanta, GA 30342
404-843-0166

Einsel, Walter
26 South Morningside Drive
Westport, CT 06880
203-226-0709

Falls, Mark
The Mark Falls Corporation
605 Lincoln Road/Suite 410
Miami Beach, FL 33319
305-532-7573

Hall, Joan
155 Bank Street, H954
New York, NY 10014
212-243-6059

Hart, Cynthia
Cynthia Hart Designer
902 Broadway Penthouse
New York, NY 10010
212-475-4660

Kagan-Batelman, Jill
47-16 39th Avenue
Sunnyside, NY 11104
718-392-3483

Klumpp, Susan
989 Vincent Ct.
Westerville, OH 43081
614-891-7593

Lang, Cecily
250 E. Royal Palm Road
Boca Raton, FL 33432
407-392-5860

Manning, Michael
Olive Jar Animation
44 White Place
Brookline, MA 02146
617-566-6699

Nichols, Susan C.
1192 Stardust Way
Royal Palm Beach, FL 33411
407-790-4413

Norby, Carol H.
Carol Norby Illustration
112 South Main
Alpine, UT 84004
801-756-1096

Otnes, Fred
26 Chalburn Road
West Redding, CT 06896
203-938-2829

Pavey, Jerry
Jerry Pavey Design & Illustration
507 Orchard Way
Silver Spring, MD 20904
301-384-3377

Saint John, Bob
320 South Street
Portsmouth, NH 03801
603-436-1567

Saksa, Cathy
Saksa Art + Design
41 Union Square West/Suite 1001
New York, NY 10003
212-255-5539

Shohet, Marti
41 Union Square West/Room 1001
New York, NY 10003
212-627-1299

Sturm, Linda K.
3 Evergreen Lane
Chappaqua, NY 10514
914-238-8318

Tarrish, Laura
123 Townsend Street/#215
San Francisco, CA 94107
415-442-1866

Vainisi, Jennine
58 Middagh Street/#16
Brooklyn, NY 11201
718-858-4914

Webb, Lizanne Elaine
Studio 22
Webster, NY 14580
716-265-4542

PAPER ENGINEERING

Cuzzi, Frank E.
Intervisual Communications
143 West 20th Street/Suite 8N
New York, NY 10011
212-989-0500
(Paper Engineering Surrounding Talking Chips)

PAPER MÂCHÉ

Selby, Bob
Providence Journal
75 Fountain Street
Providence, RI 02902
401-277-7257

Sievers, Lee & Mary
Sievers' Studio
5516 Queen Avenue South
Minneapolis, MN 55410
612-929-1726

PAPER POP-UPS

UNITED STATES

Alpert, Olive
Olive Alpert/Design
9511 Shore Road/Apt.111
Brooklyn, NY 11209
718-833-3092

Borden, Kinley W.
1305 Grandview Street
Dunmore, PA 18509
717-253-7901

Cuzzi, Frank E.
Intervisual Communications
143 West 20th Street/Suite 8N
New York, NY 10011
212-989-0500

Hahn, Eileen
8 Hillwood Road
East Brunswick, NJ 08816
908-390-4188

Ives, William R.
Ives Design
7930 Barnes Street/Apt. B-4
Philadelphia, PA 19111
215-742-9947

Kritchman/Knuteson, Joan
Advertising Art Studios, Inc.
710 North Plankinton
Milwaukee, WI 53203
414-276-6306

Lõse, Hal
Hal Associates-Toad Hall
533 W. Hortter Street
Philadelphia, PA 19119
215-849-7635

Murakami, Tak
1535 W. Juneway Terrace
Chicago, IL 60626
312-764-7845

Pauly, Mary Jo
Lychnobite Design
611 West Street N.
Jordan, MN 55352
612-492-6846

Rixford, Ellen
Ellen Rixford Studio
308 West 97th Street/#71
New York, NY 10025
212-865-5686

Saint John, Bob
320 South Street
Portsmouth, NH 03801
603-436-1567

Simonetti, John
Dimensional Design
8179 University Drive/Suite 93
Tamarac, FL 33321
305-720-9054

Tyrrell, Susan
Ruby Shoes Studio
124 Watertown Street
Watertown, MA 02172
617-923-9965

Webb, Lizanne Elaine
Studio 22
PO Box 432
Webster, NY 14580
716-265-4542

PAPER SCULPTURE

CANADA

Valera, Dennis
157 Jameson Avenue/307
Toronto, Ontario Canada M6K2Y4
416-535-0242

DENMARK

Thaae, Søren
3-D Illustrations
38 Auroravej, DK-2610
Copenhagen, Denmark
011-45-31411411

UNITED STATES

Alavezos, Gus
2215 Ptarmigan Lane
Colorado Springs, CO 80918
719-594-4100

Allen, Pat
Kathy Braun Represents
75 Water Street
San Francisco, CA 94133
415-775-3366

Alpert, Olive
Olive Alpert/Design
9511 Shore Road/Apt.111
Brooklyn, NY 11209
718-833-3092

Ash, Susan
Ravenhill Represents
4816 Jarboe Street
Kansas City, MO 64112
913-677-0028

Bandle, Johnna
J B Illustration
7726 Noland Rd.
Lenexa, KS 66216
913-962-9595

Bass, Marilyn
Bass & Goldman, Inc.
RD 3 Gypsy Trail Road
Carmel, NY 10512
914-225-8611

Berglund, Cindy
Cindy Berglund Illus. & Design
5275 E. Lake Beach Court
Shoreview, MN 55126
612-490-5141

Billin-Frye, Paige
Paige Billin-Frye Illustration
216 Walnut Street NW
Washington, D.C. 20012
202-291-3105

Borden, Kinley W.
1305 Grandview Street
Dunmore, PA 18509
717-253-7901

PAPER SCULPTURE
(Continued)

UNITED STATES

Cable, Jerry
Jerry Cable Design
133 Kuhl Road
Flemington, NJ 08822
908-788-8673/Fax 908-788-8673

Cuzzi, Frank E.
Intervisual Communications
143 West 20th Street/Suite 8N
New York, NY 10011
212-989-0500

DeCerchio, Joseph
JDC Designs
62 Marlborough Avenue
Marlton, NJ 08053
609-596-0598

DeLoy, Dee
Newstart Art
8166 Jellison Street
Orlando, FL 32825
407-273-8365

Finewood, Bill
Art Works, Inc.
605 Main Street
East Rochester, NY 14445
716-377-3126

Graham, Jack
Graham Illustration
4415 E. Ashurst Drive
Phoenix, AZ 85044
602-759-9353

Hazlerig, Mark L.
F/X Illustration
3619 Washburn Street
Columbus, OH 43213
614-239-9290

Klumpp, Susan
989 Vincent Ct.
Westerville, OH 43081
614-891-7593

Kritchman/Knuteson, Joan
Advertising Art Studios, Inc.
710 North Plankinton
Milwaukee, WI 53203
414-276-6306

Lõse, Hal
Hal Associates-Toad Hall
533 W. Hortter Street
Philadelphia, PA 19119
215-849-7635

Luch, Phyllis
Luch Studios
2614 Westshire Drive
Salt Lake City, UT 84119
801-968-1382

Manning, Michael
Olive Jar Animation
44 White Place
Brookline, MA 02146
617-566-6699

Miller, Bill
Bill Miller/Illustration
1355 N. Sandburg Terrace
Suite 2002 D
Chicago, IL 60610
312-787-4093

Moe-Duffeck, Suzanne
Nachreiner-Boie Art Factory
925 Elm Grove Road
Elm Grove, WI 53122
414-785-1940

Monahan, Leo
1912 Hilton Drive
Burbank, CA 91504
818-843-6115/818-842-8866

Murakami, Tak
1535 W. Juneway Terrace
Chicago, IL 60626
312-764-7845

Nishinaka, Jeff
362 N. Crescent Hts. Blvd.
Los Angeles, CA 90048
213-655-5302

Nitzberg, Andrew
240 E. 27th Street
New York, NY 10016
212-684-6745

Noda, Ajin
Ajin Noda & Associates, Inc.
446 West 49th Street/#1B
New York, NY 10019
212-333-7377

Paperny, Vladimir
Vladimir Paperny & Associates
1114 12th Street/#101
Santa Monica, CA 90403
213-393-7564

Pauly, Mary Jo
Lychnobite Design
611 West Street N.
Jordan, MN 55352
612-492-6846

Pavey, Jerry
Jerry Pavey Design & Illustration
507 Orchard Way
Silver Spring, MD 20904
301-384-3377

Rixford, Ellen
Ellen Rixford Studio
308 West 97th Street/#71
New York, NY 10025
212-865-5686

Spencer, Kimberly
Salon Enterprises
1739 Four Mile Road, NE
Grand Rapids, MI 49505
616-363-4000

Sturm, Linda K.
3 Evergreen Lane
Chappaqua, NY 10514
914-238-8318

Suyeoka, George
699 Sheridan Road
Evanston, IL 60202
708-475-1090

Traynor, Elizabeth
Elizabeth Traynor Illustration
Rt. 12, Box 32, Barbee Chapel Rd.
Chapel Hill, NC 27514
919-968-6573

Tyrrell, Susan
Ruby Shoes Studio
124 Watertown Street
Watertown, MA 02172
617-923-9965

Tysko, Lisa
361 Design Group
361 Nassau Street
Princeton, NJ 08540
609-921-3610

Vitsky, Sally
Sally Vitsky Illustration
4116 Bromley Lane
Richmond, VA 23221
804-359-4726

Webb, Lizanne Elaine
Studio 22
PO Box 432
Webster, NY 14580
716-265-4542

White, Meg
1322 Ridgeway Avenue
New Albany, IN 47150
812-945-2901

Williams, Toby
Toby Williams Illustration
84 Franklin Street
Watertown, MA 02172
617-924-2406

Workman, Jef
Bird In The Hand Studio
310 Carmel Avenue
Pacific Grove, CA 93950
408-372-9010

PLASTER

UNITED STATES

Arroyo, Andrea
Andrea Arroyo Studio
PO Box 1472
New York, NY 10009-8904
212-477-2485

Bono, Mary M.
288 Graham Avenue
Brooklyn, NY 11211
718-387-3774

Burns, Sean
Olive Jar Animation
44 White Place
Brookline, MA 02146
617-566-6699

Daley, Carolyn
4665 Refugee Road/Apt.3H
Columbus, OH 43232
614-759-0209

Hazlerig, Mark L.
F/X Illustration
3619 Washburn Street
Columbus, OH 43213
614-239-9290

Klumpp, Susan
989 Vincent CT.
Westerville, OH 43081
614-891-7593

Murakami, Tak
1535 W. Juneway Terrace
Chicago, IL 60626
312-764-7845

Otnes, Fred
26 Chalburn Road
West Redding, CT 06896
203-938-2829

Rixford, Ellen
Ellen Rixford Studio
308 West 97th Street/#71
New York, NY 10025
212-865-5686

Saint John, Bob
320 South Street
Portsmouth, NH 03801
603-436-1567

Seman, Ron
The Object Works
12 Eighth Street
Pittsburgh, PA 15222
412-261-3513

Sturm, Linda K.
3 Evergreen Lane
Chappaqua, NY 10514
914-238-8318

PLASTIC SCULPTURE

ENGLAND

Fouts, Nancy
Shirt Sleeve Studio
52 Oakley Square
The Old Vicarage
London, England NW1 1NJ
071-388-6491

UNITED STATES

Aristovulos, Nick
16 East 30th Street
New York, NY 10016
212-725-2454

Arroyo, Andrea
Andrea Arroyo Studio
PO Box 1472
New York, NY 10009-8904
212-477-2485

Bandle, Johnna
J B Illustration
7726 Noland Rd.
Lenexa, KS 66216
913-962-9595

Bono, Mary M.
288 Graham Avenue
Brooklyn, NY 11211
718-387-3774

Carlton, Chuck
Axiom, Inc.
120 So. Brook Street
Louisville KY 40202
502-584-7666

Daley, Carolyn
4665 Refugee Road/Apt.3H
Columbus, OH 43232
614-759-0209

Emmott, Bob
Emmott Photography, Inc.
700 South 10th Street
Philadelphia, PA 19147
215-925-2773

Field, Bob
336 Washington Street
Brookline, MA 02146
617-232-2230

Finewood, Bill
Art Works, Inc.
605 Main Street
East Rochester, NY 14445
716-377-3126

Grimmett, Douglass
1013 Carmel Church Road
Chapel Hill, NC 27514
919-967-6841

Hazlerig, Mark L.
F/X Illustration
3619 Washburn Street
Columbus, OH 43213
614-239-9290

Klumpp, Susan
989 Vincent Ct.
Westerville, OH 43081
614-891-7593

Manning, Michael
Olive Jar Animation
44 White Place
Brookline, MA 02146
617-566-6699

Murakami, Tak
1535 W. Juneway Terrace
Chicago, IL 60626
312-764-7845

Nazz, James
42 Steyvesant Street
New York, NY 10003
212-228-9713

Rixford, Ellen
Ellen Rixford Studio
308 West 97th Street/#71
New York, NY 10025
212-865-5686

Saint John, Bob
320 South Street
Portsmouth, NH 03801
603-436-1567

Sanders, James
Get Up And Gourmet. Inc.
2066 Lyric Avenue
Los Angeles, CA 90039
213-669-1879

Schmeelk, William
Wellington Enterprises
55 Railroad Avenue
Garnerville, NY 10923
914-429-3377

Seman, Ron
The Object Works
12 Eighth Street
Pittsburgh, PA 15222
412-261-3513

Yurkiw, Mark
Mark Yurkiw Ltd.
568 Broadway/Suite 605
New York, NY 10012
212-226-6338

Ziegler, Kathleen
Dimensional Illustrators, Inc.
362 2nd Street Pike/Suite 112
Southampton, PA 18966
215-953-1415/Fax 215-953-1697

POLYURETHANE FOAMS

Klumpp, Susan
989 Vincent CT.
Westerville, OH 43081
614-891-7593

PUPPETS

Rixford, Ellen
Ellen Rixford Studio
308 West 97th Street/#71
New York, NY 10025
212-865-5686

SAMPLERS

Bobin, Chris
5 East 17th Street/6th FL
New York, NY 10003
212-691-2821/212-475-7268

Cusack, Margaret
124 Hoyt Street
Brooklyn, NY 11217-2215
718-237-0145

SAND SCULPTURE

Vanderpluym, Todd
Sand Sculptors International
425 Via Anita
Redondo Beach, CA 90277
213-372-5559

SOFT SCULPTURE

Lallky-Seibert, Bonnie
161 N.E. 38 Street/#19-B
Ft. Lauderdale, FL 33334
305-564-3259

WOOD CARVING

Blauers, Nancy
50 Walnut Street
Stratford, CT 06497
203-377-6109

Rasmussen, Bonnie
A.Art/B.Rasmussen, Ltd.
8828 Pendleton
St. Louis, MO 63144
314-962-1842/Fax 314-962-4816

WOOD SCULPTURE

CANADA

Fleming, Joe
Joe Fleming Illustration
487 Mortimer Avenue
Toronto, Canada M4J2G6
416-466-0630

ENGLAND

Fowler, Malcolm
Shirt Sleeve Studio
52 Oakley Square
The Old Vicarage
London, England NW1 1NJ
071-388-6491

UNITED STATES

Alpert, Olive
Olive Alpert/Design
9511 Shore Road/Apt.111
Brooklyn, NY 11209
718-833-3092

Arroyo, Andrea
Andrea Arroyo Studio
PO Box 1472
New York, NY 10009-8904
212-477-2485

Blauers, Nancy
50 Walnut Street
Stratford, CT 06497
203-377-6109

Burns, Sean
Olive Jar Animation
44 White Place
Brookline, MA 02146
617-566-6699

Carlton, Chuck
Axiom, Inc.
120 So. Brook Street
Louisville KY 40202
502-584-7666

Christensen, Gayle
1026 Maywood Lane
Martinez, CA 94553
415-943-8161

Einsel, Walter
26 South Morningside Drive
Westport, CT 06880
203-226-0709

Emmott, Bob
Emmott Photography, Inc.
700 South 10th Street
Philadelphia, PA 19147
215-925-2773

Finewood, Bill
Art Works, Inc.
605 Main Street
East Rochester, NY 14445
716-377-3126

Hazlerig, Mark L.
F/X Illustration
3619 Washburn Street
Columbus, OH 43213
614-239-9290

Klumpp, Susan
989 Vincent Ct.
Westerville, OH 43081
614-891-7593

Murakami, Tak
1535 W. Juneway Terrace
Chicago, IL 60626
312-764-7845

WOOD SCULPTURE
(Continued)

UNITED STATES

Nazz, James
42 Steyvesant Street
New York, NY 10003
212-228-9713

Pavey, Jerry
Jerry Pavey Design & Illustration
507 Orchard Way
Silver Spring, MD 20904
301-384-3377

Rasmussen, Bonnie
A.Art/B.Rasmussen, Ltd.
8828 Pendleton
St. Louis, MO 63144
314-962-1842/Fax 314-962-4816

Rixford, Ellen
Ellen Rixford Studio
308 West 97th Street/#71
New York, NY 10025
212-865-5686

Saint John, Bob
320 South Street
Portsmouth, NH 03801
603-436-1567

Schmeelk, William
Wellington Enterprises
55 Railroad Avenue
Garnerville, NY 10923
914-429-3377

Seman, Ron
The Object Works
12 Eighth Street
Pittsburgh, PA 15222
412-261-3513

Sturm, Linda K.
3 Evergreen Lane
Chappaqua, NY 10514
914-238-8318

Suyeoka, George
699 Sheridan Road
Evanston, IL 60202
708-475-1090

CANADA

Chatwin, Robert
3-D Illustrator
25 Winnett Avenue
Toronto, Ontario Canada M6C 3L2
416-657-8133

Elsom, Vicky
Vicky Elsom Design
95 Lawton Blvd/607
Toronto, Ontario/Canada M4V 128
416-489-6453

Fleming, Joe
Joe Fleming Illustration
487 Mortimer Avenue
Toronto, Canada M4J2G6
416-466-0630

Valera, Dennis
157 Jameson Avenue/307
Toronto, Ontario Canada M6K2Y4
416-535-0242

DENMARK

Thaae, Søren
3-D Illustrations
38 Auroravej, DK-2610
Copenhagen, Denmark
011-45-31411411

ENGLAND

Fouts, Nancy
Shirt Sleeve Studio
52 Oakley Square
The Old Vicarage
London, England NW1 1NJ
071-388-6491

Fowler, Malcolm
Shirt Sleeve Studio
52 Oakley Square
The Old Vicarage
London, England NW1 1NJ
071-388-6491

GERMANY

Kiel, Achim
Pencil Corporate Art
Kulturzentrum Rundbogen
Heinrich-Buessing-Hof D-3300
Braunschweig Lower Saxony/Germany
0531-72964

SCOTLAND

Watson, Douglas
2 Leadervale Road
Edinburgh, Scotland UK EH16 6PA
031-664-2524

SWITZERLAND

Gasser, Philip
Kraftstr, 11
Basel, Switzerland 4056
061-322-1412

Van der Bie, Esther
Kloesterlistutz #2
Bern, Switzerland 3013
031-428-572

UNITED STATES

Ajin
Ajin Noda & Associates, Inc.
446 West 49th Street/#1B
New York, NY 10019
212-333-7377

Alavezos, Gus
2215 Ptarmigan Lane
Colorado Springs, CO 80918
719-594-4100

Allen, Pat
Kathy Braun Represents
75 Water Street
San Francisco, CA 94133
415-775-3366

Alpert, Olive
Olive Alpert/Design
9511 Shore Road/Apt.111
Brooklyn, NY 11209
718-833-3092

Aristovulos, Nick
16 East 30th Street
New York, NY 10016
212-725-2454

Arroyo, Andrea
Andrea Arroyo Studio
PO Box 1472
New York, NY 10009-8904
212-477-2485

Ash, Susan
Ravenhill Represents
4816 Jarboe Street
Kansas City, MO 64112
913-677-0028

Bandle, Johnna
J B Illustration
7726 Noland Rd.
Lenexa, KS 66216
913-962-9595

Bartlett, Christopher
Bartlett & Associates
2211B Woodbox Lane
Baltimore, MD 21209
301-484-1906

Bass, Marilyn
Bass & Goldman, Inc.
RD 3 Gypsy Trail Road
Carmel, NY 10512
914-225-8611

Baum, Susan
123 Palisade Street
Dobbs Ferry, NY 10522
914-693-5143

Berglund, Cindy
Cindy Berglund Illus. & Design
5275 E. Lake Beach Court
Shoreview, MN 55126
612-490-5141

Berman, Jim
Olive Jar Animation
44 White Place
Brookline, MA 02146
617-566-6699

Berman, Simi
Box 58
Chesterfield, NH 03443
603-256-8477

Billin-Frye, Paige
Paige Billin-Frye Illustration
216 Walnut Street NW
Washington, D.C. 20012
202-291-3105

Blauers, Nancy
50 Walnut Street
Stratford, CT 06497
203-377-6109

Bobin, Chris
5 East 17th Street/6th FL
New York, NY 10003
212-691-2821/212-475-7268

Bono, Mary M.
288 Graham Avenue
Brooklyn, NY 11211
718-387-3774

Borden, Kinley W.
1305 Grandview Street
Dunmore, PA 18509
717-253-7901

Botsis, Peter
Botsis Studio
2467 Culver Road
Rochester, NY 14609
716-288-7080

Browne, Rob
541 Winterberry Way
San Jose, CA 95129
408-255-8843

Burnett, Lindy
476 Loridans Drive
Atlanta, GA 30342
404-843-0166

Burns, Sean
Olive Jar Animation
44 White Place
Brookline, MA 02146
617-566-6699

Cable, Jerry
Jerry Cable Design
133 Kuhl Road
Flemington, NJ 08822
908-788-8673/Fax 908-788-8673

Carlton, Chuck
Axiom, Inc.
120 S. Brook Street
Louisville, KY 40202
502-584-7666

Chaden, Tina
232 E. 12th Street
New York, NY 10003
212-475-6784

Christensen, Gayle
1026 Maywood Lane
Martinez, CA 94553
415-943-8161

Cook, Anne
Anne Cook Textile Art & Illus.
96 Rollingwood Drive
San Rafael, CA 94901
415-454-5799

Corfield, Marie
48 Sylvan Place
Nutley, NJ 07110
201-667-8071

Cusack, Margaret
124 Hoyt Street
Brooklyn, NY 11217-2215
718-237-0145

Cuzzi, Frank E.
Intervisual Communications
143 West 20th Street/Suite 8N
New York, NY 10011
212-989-0500

Daley, Carolyn
4665 Refugee Road/Apt.3H
Columbus, OH 43232
614-759-0209

DeCerchio, Joseph
JDC Designs
62 Marlborough Avenue
Marlton, NJ 08053
609-596-0598

DeLoy, Dee
Newstart Art
8166 Jellison Street
Orlando, FL 32825
407-273-8365

Downer, Jim
Olive Jar Animation
44 White Place
Brookline, MA 02146
617-566-6699

Einsel, Walter
26 South Morningside Drive
Westport, CT 06880
203-226-0709

Eldridge, Gary
163 South Center Street
Lowell, MI 49331
616-897-6668

Emmott, Bob
Emmott Photography, Inc.
700 South 10th Street
Philadelphia, PA 19147
215-925-2773

Falls, Mark
The Mark Falls Corporation
605 Lincoln Road/Suite 410
Miami Beach, FL 33319
305-532-7573

Field, Bob
336 Washington Street
Brookline, MA 02146
617-232-2230

Finewood, Bill
Art Works, Inc.
605 Main Street
East Rochester, NY 14445
716-377-3126

Foord, Mimi
Smaller Than Life Productions
1595 Stanford Street
Concord, CA 94519
415-680-0493

Frick, Thomas
227 Doris Avenue
Baltimore, MD 21225
301-789-3045

Frizzell, Mark
P.O. Box 3176
Woburn, MA 01888
617-933-0805

Gay-Kassel, Doreen
24a Chestnut Ct.
Princeton, NJ 08540
609-497-0783

Goodman, Michael L.
1922 Windingridge Drive
Richmond, VA 23233
804-771-9331

Graham, Jack
Graham Illustration
4415 E. Ashurst Drive
Phoenix, AZ 85044
602-759-9353

Grimmett, Douglass
1013 Carmel Church Road
Chapel Hill, NC 27514
919-967-6841

Hahn, Eileen
8 Hillwood Road
East Brunswick, NJ 08816
908-390-4188

Hall, Joan
155 Bank Street, H954
New York, NY 10014
212-243-6059

Hart, Cynthia
Cynthia Hart Designer
902 Broadway Penthouse
New York, NY 10010
212-475-4660

Hazlerig, Mark L.
F/X Illustration
3619 Washburn Street
Columbus, OH 43213
614-239-9290

Hoffman, Joanne
Hoffman Studios
826 Kater Street
Philadelphia, PA 19147
215-928-9365

Ives, William R.
Ives Design
7930 Barnes Street/Apt. B-4
Philadelphia, PA 19111
215-742-9947

Jeffers, Kathy
151 West 19th Street/3rdFL
New York, NY 10011
212-255-5196

Kagan-Batelman, Jill
47-16 39th Avenue
Sunnyside, NY 11104
718-392-3483

Klumpp, Susan
989 Vincent Ct.
Westerville, OH 43081
614-891-7593

Koudis, Nick
Nick Koudis Studio
40 East 23rd Street
New York, NY 10010
212-475-2802

Kritchman/Knuteson, Joan
Advertising Art Studios, Inc.
710 North Plankinton
Milwaukee, WI 53203
414-276-6306

Lallky-Seibert, Bonnie
161 N.E. 38 Street/#19-B
Ft. Lauderdale, FL 33334
305-564-3259

LaMantia, Joe
LaMantia Studio
820 West Howe Street
Bloomington, IN 47403
812-332-2667

Lang, Cecily
250 E Royal Palm Road
Boca Raton, FL 33432
407-392-5860

Lemmon, John
John Lemmon Films
1216 Pinecrest Avenue
Charlotte, NC 28205
704-532-1944

Littman, Rosemary
Rosemary's Cakes
299 Rutland Avenue
Teaneck, NJ 07666
201-833-3092

Lōse, Hal
Hal Associates-Toad Hall
533 W. Hortter Street
Philadelphia, PA 19119
215-849-7635

Luch, Phyllis
Luch Studios
2614 Westshire Drive
Salt Lake City, UT 84119
801-968-1382

Manning, Michael
Olive Jar Animation
44 White Place
Brookline, MA 02146
617-566-6699

Maraschiello, Frank
520 2nd Avenue
New York, NY 10016
212-889-6012

Marisol
c/o Time Magazine Art Dept.
1271 Avenue of the Americas
New York, NY 10020
212-522-4769

McNeel, Richard
530 Valley Road/#2G
Upper Montclair, NJ 07043
201-509-2255

Mikec, Larry
Art Factory
925 Elm Grove Road
Elm Grove, WI 53122
414-785-1940

Miller, Bill
Bill Miller/Illustration
1355 N. Sandburg Terrace
Suite 2002 D
Chicago, IL 60610
312-787-4093

Moe-Duffeck, Suzanne
Nachreiner-Boie Art Factory
925 Elm Grove Road
Elm Grove, WI 53122
414-785-1940

Molampy, Scott
Geppetto Soft Sculpture & Display
107 Lexington Avenue/4th FL
Brooklyn, NY 11238
718-398-9792

Monahan, Leo
1912 Hilton Drive
Burbank, CA 91504
818-843-6115/818-842-8866

Morsette, Zoe
Mark Yurkiw Ltd.
568 Broadway/Suite 605
New York, NY 10012
212-226-6338

Muhs, Jeffery
Mark Yurkiw Ltd.
568 Broadway/Suite 605
New York, NY 10012
212-226-6338

Murakami, Tak
1535 W. Juneway Terrace
Chicago, IL 60626
312-764-7845

Nachreiner, Tom
Art Factory
925 Elm Grove Road
Elm Grove, WI 53122
414-785-1940

Nazz, James
42 Steyvesant Street
New York, NY 10003
212-228-9713

Nichols, Susan C.
1192 Stardust Way
Royal Palm Beach, FL 33411
407-790-4413

Nishinaka, Jeff
362 N. Crescent Hts. Blvd.
Los Angeles, CA 90048
213-655-5302

Nitzberg, Andrew
240 E. 27th Street
New York, NY 10016
212-684-6745

Norby, Carol H.
Carol Norby Illustration
112 South Main
Alpine, UT 84004
801-756-1096

Otnes, Fred
26 Chalburn Road
West Redding, CT 06896
203-938-2829

Paperny, Vladimir
Vladimir Paperny & Associates
1114 12th Street/#101
Santa Monica, CA 90403
213-393-7564

Pauly, Mary Jo
Lychnobite Design
611 West Street N.
Jordan, MN 55352
612-492-6846

Pavey, Jerry
Jerry Pavey Design & Illustration
507 Orchard Way
Silver Spring, MD 20904
301-384-3377

Rasmussen, Bonnie
A.Art/B.Rasmussen, Ltd.
8828 Pendleton
St. Louis, MO 63144
314-962-1842/Fax 314-962-4816

Rixford, Ellen
Ellen Rixford Studio
308 West 97th Street/#71
New York, NY 10025
212-865-5686

Rosinski, Mike
John Lemmon Films
1216 Pinecrest Avenue
Charlotte, NC 28205
704-532-1944

Saint John, Bob
320 South Street
Portsmouth, NH 03801
603-436-1567

Saksa, Cathy
Saksa Art + Design
41 Union Square West/Suite 1001
New York, NY 10003
212-255-5539

Sanders, James
Get Up And Gourmet. Inc.
2066 Lyric Avenue
Los Angeles, CA 90039
213-669-1879

Schmeelk, William
Wellington Enterprises
55 Railroad Avenue
Garnerville, NY 10923
914-429-3377

Selby, Bob
Providence Journal
75 Fountain Street
Providence, RI 02902
401-277-7257

Seman, Ron
The Object Works
12 Eighth Street
Pittsburgh, PA 15222
412-261-3513

Shohet, Marti
41 Union Square West/Room 1001
New York, NY 10003
212-627-1299

Sievers, Lee & Mary
Sievers' Studio
5516 Queen Avenue South
Minneapolis, MN 55410
612-929-1726

Simonetti, John
Dimensional Design
8179 University Drive/Suite 93
Tamarac, FL 33321
305-720-9054

Spencer, Kimberly
Salon Enterprises
1739 Four Mile Road, NE
Grand Rapids, MI 49505
616-363-4000

Steiner, Joan
Bate Road, Box 292, RD 1
Craryville, NY 12521
518-851-7199

Sturm, Linda K.
3 Evergreen Lane
Chappaqua, NY 10514
914-238-8318

Suyeoka, George
699 Sheridan Road
Evanston, IL 60202
708-475-1090

Swenarton, Gordon
Falcone & Associates
13 Watchung Avenue
Chatham, NJ 07928
201-635-2900

Tarrish, Laura
123 Townsend Street/#215
San Francisco, CA 94107
415-442-1866

Traynor, Elizabeth
Elizabeth Traynor Illustration
Rt. 12, Box 32, Barbee Chapel Rd.
Chapel Hill, NC 27514
919-968-6573

Tyrrell, Susan
Ruby Shoes Studio
124 Watertown Street
Watertown, MA 02172
617-923-9965

Tysko, Lisa
361 Design Group
361 Nassau Street
Princeton, NJ 08540
609-921-3610

Vainisi, Jennine
58 Middagh Street/#16
Brooklyn, NY 11201
718-858-4914

Vanderpluym, Todd
Sand Sculptors International
425 Via Anita
Redondo Beach, CA 90277
213-372-5559

Vinton, Will
Will Vinton Productions, Inc
1400 NW 22nd Avenue
Portland, OR 97210
503-225-1130

Vitsky, Sally
Sally Vitsky Illustration
4116 Bromley Lane
Richmond, VA 23221
804-359-4726

Wagner, James & Shirley
Art Factory
925 Elm Grove Road
Elm Grove, WI 53122
414-785-1940

Webb, Lizanne Elaine
Studio 22
PO Box 432
Webster, NY 14580
716-265-4542

White, Meg
1322 Ridgeway Avenue
New Albany, IN 47150
812-945-2901

Williams, Toby
Toby Williams Illustration
84 Franklin Street
Watertown, MA 02172
617-924-2406

Workman, Jef
Bird In The Hand Studio
310 Carmel Avenue
Pacific Grove, CA 93950
408-372-9010

Yurkiw, Mark
Mark Yurkiw Ltd.
568 Broadway/Suite #605
New York, NY 10012
212-226-6338

Ziegler, Kathleen
Dimensional Illustrators, Inc.
362 2nd Street Pike/Suite 112
Southampton, PA 18966
215-953-1415/Fax 215-953-1697

3-D ILLUSTRATORS

ANIMATION STUDIOS